WORKING TOWARD SAINTHOOD

Daily Reflections for Lent

ALICE CAMILLE

TWENTY THIRD *23rd*
PUBLICATIONS
www.23rdpublications.com

For my Godparents,
Irene Vivino and Andrew Yenolevage,
dear first witnesses in faith

For the Scripture verses quoted on these pages, I've used *The Message: Catholic/Ecumenical Edition* by Eugene Peterson and William Griffin (Chicago: ACTA Publications, 2013). Exuberant, sometimes cheeky, never sacrificing the spirit for the mere letter of the text, *The Message* provides a fresh response to the familiar lenten passages.

Also, the daily readings for Lent are the same each year. But the Sunday readings follow a three-year cycle: A, B, or C. In order to make this book useful every year, I've included three reflections for the Sundays of Lent. Check your parish bulletin or Catholic calendar to determine which year of the Sunday cycle we're following this year.

Twenty-Third Publications
1 Montauk Avenue, Suite 200, New London, CT 06320
(860) 437-3012 ◆ (800) 321-0411◆ www.23rdpublications.com

ISBN: 978-1-58595-924-2
Library of Congress Catalog Card Number: 2013949033
Printed in the U.S.A.

CONTENTS

INTRODUCTION

.

HEROES ARE HUGE IN POP CULTURE. Compared with them, our lives can seem so plain vanilla. Heroes help us imagine a reality where transcendence is possible and the sky's the limit! Heroes show us how that's done.

In the realm of sanctity, saints inhabit hero territory. They crash through mortal barriers of temptation, sickness, and fear. They embrace an immortality made more exciting because it's real. Their virtue is so strong, it can't be overcome and can't die. They wear bonnets of light because they never hid their lamps under a bushel. The world is different because the saints lived among us. And live among us still, if we understand the story correctly.

We can be like them. Baptism inaugurated our life of sanctity. Each year Lent provides us with forty days to dust off our baptismal promises and to polish our haloes, tarnished by another year of business as usual. Our inner saint needs exercise to become our default self.

The season of Lent is called many things: a journey, a challenge, a penance, an opportunity. I approach it as a landscape. As we view the rolling gospel scenery of these weeks, we engage the twin activities of contemplation and decision. The focus moves from desert to city, from solitude to community, from temptation to dedication, and from personal accomplishment to radical trust in what only God can do.

We don't come to this season to admire the landscape, as one does a painting in a museum. Lent is a totally immersive environment. We enter it body and soul, and each year find this space of forty days a different experience. How can this be? The biblical geography, from wilderness to Jerusalem, remains the same. But we're not. The desert changes because our temptations are unique to each season of our lives. Community is different because our involvement increases or withdraws, depending on our circumstances. What we accomplish in this environment depends on what we give up or take on here. Above all, the lenten landscape proves wonderful or dreadful, welcome or forbidding, as a result of our relationship to God these days. Do we begin Lent this time as friends of God or strangers; are we lately more partners or prisoners of the divine purposes?

Some years, Lent affirms our sense of discipline. Other Lents are shocking proof of how meager our ability is to say no to self. Some seasons are highlighted by intimacy in prayer and growth in charity. Others underscore the gap between God's will and ours, and the poverty of our love. Yet each Lent is a success. Each teaches us who we are and reminds us who we're invited to be. The only useless Lent is the one not conscientiously engaged. To sit out a Lent is to miss the next lesson in sainthood.

Chances are, you and I will still have some tarnish left on our haloes come Easter. Our future canonization won't yet be a sure thing. Don't be discouraged. Titles are garnish. Consecrating each day to love is what matters. The world needs saints now as much as ever. So let's get out there, superheroes! They may not know us by our capes, but they will know us by our love.

ASH WEDNESDAY

Gather

Blow the ram's horn trumpet in Zion!
Declare a day of repentance, a holy fast day.
Call a public meeting. Get everyone there.

JOEL 2:15

LENT STARTS ON AN ORDINARY DAY OF THE WEEK. Not
even a holy day, mind you. Yet it boasts the biggest church attendance of any day except Good Friday, another voluntary observance. Why do folks seem to want their ashes more than the
sacraments? Maybe because we're pretty sure we don't deserve
holy things—but we do deserve what's coming to us.

While this isn't wrong, it's not the whole story. We're mortal,

which means we're going to die. Death is a given because sin is. Our world is broken and so are we. It's the oldest story in the Bible. But it's not the final word on reality, thanks be to God.

Ashes remind us that we're dust. They also mark us willing to "repent, and believe the good news." If the bad news is that this life does end, the good news is that any of us can choose the new, high, better, true life. We traditionally call it "the life to come." We could just as easily say: the life that's already in motion, waiting for us to sign up and join in.

Ashes aren't a magical mark. But they are a notary seal on the smudged contract of our intentions. Every contract needs witnesses. So we gather on this quiet, off-the-grid midweek day and start Lent together. Together, as a family of faith, we say: hey, we know who we are and what we are. We know our chances of getting out of this world alive. We're prepared to aim higher, go deeper. We want to get it right this time.

This odd Wednesday gathering shakes up our spiritual routines and tells us something unusual's going on. We're going to fast and pray and share. We're going to tell the truth and make some promises. We're in this together, as church. This isn't "my" Lent. It's ours. So let's do Lent as couples, families, friends, and community. See you in church.

Idea of the day

I can't be church alone. Who's part of my faith family? How real is this support? How do I employ its resources, or how might I invest in it to make it stronger? I dedicate this day of fast and abstinence to my faith family.

Choose

Look at what I've done for you today:
I've placed in front of you Life and Good, Death and Evil.
Choose life so that you and your children will live.

DEUTERONOMY 30:15, 19B

WE SIT WITH CHOICES DAILY. The baloney sandwich or the healthy salad? Another hour of mindless television or fifteen minutes of spiritual reading? React to the needy child and pestering coworker with an irritating snap or gentle attention? Engage in conversation to draw attention to myself or to share in the gift of someone else?

Mostly our decisions are small and forgettable. Whether I say something encouraging in this moment or nothing at all may seem inconsequential. But each decision is a step down a path, the ending of which is cumulatively significant. One gained pound becomes twenty. Tonight's snippy remark becomes the one that finally breaks a heart. Too many monologues find us one day alone and ignored.

I know the sort of person I don't like to be around: cynical, demanding, moody, unkind, ungenerous. How often do my choices tip me in the direction of that personality?

The choice Moses hands the Israelites on the verge of the Promised Land still applies today: life and good, or death and evil? It's pretty clear which is which. When we neglect to make a conscious choice, we slip into habits unexamined and familiar.

When in choosing mode, however, I slow down. Don't react; act. Choosing to act involves about thirty extra seconds. I take a breath, close my eyes, sit down. I collect my thoughts and lay them out mentally in front of me. I sift through feelings and intentions with equal respect, acknowledging frankly the frustration alongside the love. I can usually come up with a better-delayed action than the reflexive one, which normally boils down to: "Leave me alone, I'm just one person!"

The liberty to choose and not to be led around by our emotions or past patterns is what we mean by free will. It distinguishes our humanity. Be human. Make real choices.

Idea of the Day

"Self control" is a fruit of the Holy Spirit (Gal 5:23). Which do I do more: exercise free will or react to input around me? Which old patterns need to be reconsidered and mastered? Which spirit lives in me today: a holy or unholy one?

Reconsider

Scrub away my guilt, soak out my sins in your laundry.
I know how bad I've been;
my sins are staring me down. **PSALM 51:2–3**

SHE SWEPT INTO THE PARISH OFFICE THAT DAY IN THE SORT OF CHAOTIC CLOUD THAT SEEMED HABITUAL. "I need ashes," the woman declared. Never mind it was Friday and Lent was already two days old all around the Catholic universe.

At the time I was a student of theology, a fervent new soldier in the ranks of ministry. Full of shiny convictions aching to be employed, I launched into an earnest presentation of The Facts. Receiving ashes is a communal ritual act peculiar to Ash

Wednesday. It being Friday, the singular wearing of ashes would mean nothing but a dirty face. Besides, no one "needs" ashes. They're not a sacrament, but a "sacramental": a helpful object or gesture that points in the direction of grace. She'd be fine without ashes this year. Really.

The woman was flattened. This young gatekeeper was denying her a mystical sign vital to her lenten experience. Just then, the pastor walked through the office. "I need ashes," the woman repeated weakly. "Follow me," the priest cheerily replied. They went into the church; he said the formula and marked her forehead. She left in joy and gratitude.

I was mad. The pastor's graciousness made me look bad. Everything I'd told that woman was right! But the priest's response made me look wrong.

I was also ashamed. My allegiance to The Facts made me forget the person. Eager to recite my lessons, I forgot that sabbaths and sacramentals are for people and not the other way around. Maybe this woman did have an incomplete understanding of ashes, but while I was judging, our pastor was listening. Anxious to correct, I failed to serve.

It was my earliest lesson in parish ministry. The right answer can't be paired with the wrong action. Catechetical answers are great for religious questions. But pastoral responses are the only reply to human need. To be of service, it's not enough to be right.

Idea of the Day

It's easy to love a rule, harder sometimes to love a person. When has my allegiance to a principle caused more harm than good? How did Jesus choose between laws and people? I dedicate this day of abstinence to those I have wronged.

Follow

Jesus said, "Come along with me."
And he did—walked away from everything and went with him.
LUKE 5:27B–28

HOW WE ADMIRE WHAT THE MAN DOES IN THIS STORY!
We congratulate him. We don't imitate him. Walking away from everything and following Jesus is what superheroes of the Bible do. It's not what real people with rents and mortgages and student loans and children do.

So here we start our bargaining: can we come along after Jesus—with a U-Haul in tow? Can we follow with a walletful of credit cards? Is it possible to sign on for a single year of discipleship like a modern volunteer corps: one and done? Is there a home-office option, where we can stay in pajamas and fuzzy slippers and still make our deadlines?

Because, let's be frank: in the twenty-first century, only a handful leave cubicles and cash registers, ranch houses and cozy apartments, to walk that road with Jesus. Apostles don't get life or health insurance, no 401Ks or SEP-IRAs. Sure, if they chip a tooth or sprain an ankle Jesus might, um, just fix it. But what are the long-term assurances in this venture? What's down the road for folks who do what that brave fellow in the gospel just did?

We have one advantage over him. We know what's at the end of the road Jesus is on. We know every inch of this journey: the wild applause and stunning condemnation, the successes and miracles. We know about mobs wanting to run Jesus off a cliff. They'll call him prophet and heretic, Son of God and devil man. His friends will dine at sumptuous tables, and sometimes there will be no place for them to sleep at night. At the far end of this trail is a cross on a lonely hill. And yes, dawn will rise on the third day after that—but we're talking a pretty intimidating "after that."

Still, this is Jesus who's inviting us. We've already determined that following him is the only way to go. We'll probably attempt it the hard way, dragging our stuff through the needle's eye and down that road. I don't know how much will be left at the far end, but if you're like me, you're going to try to carry your baggage as far as you can.

Idea of the Day
What's easy to let go of, and what's hard? What may be holding me back from taking the next step?

Persevere

Next Jesus was taken into the wild by the Spirit for the Test.
The Devil was ready to give it. **MATTHEW 4:1**

"PATIENCE IS A VIRTUE," MY MOTHER ALWAYS SAYS. It's a virtue I don't have in large quantities. So life is determined to teach me how it goes. Still, I'm not one who ascribes to the theory that God is spending all of human history testing us like kids who throw bugs in a jar, watching to see what they'll do with their options and poking a stick in once in a while to stir things up. That seems demeaning to the Almighty, and not especially loving to us.

God doesn't have to test us. Living is test enough. In an ex-

istence full of options, we have to pick a few. And then we have to deal with the results of our choices. Trouble is, everyone around us is also making choices, some better and some worse. Some a whole lot worse. And in ways that a science underachiever like me will never fully appreciate, there's also an interaction between our choices and the natural world that stirs things up much more fatefully than kids poking bugs with a stick. Some of these decisions result in disease or natural disasters. Finally, some terrible things happen for reasons we're at a loss to explain. Maybe there's some sort of spiritual causality that can't be described better than Genesis chapter three. Evil begets evil like a serpent influencing us in our weakest hours, whispering empty promises to those eager to believe them.

In some corners of the world—ghettos, war zones, prisons, brothels, as well as the privacy of some homes and hearts—evil inhabits the space for so long it becomes a substantial, tangible presence. Maybe such incarnate evil is enough to drag planets out of alignment, darken stars, alter weather patterns, and change activity on the cellular level. Who knows? Whatever the final reasons, it remains that great evil and great suffering are in this world and we'll come face to face with both. Are we prepared to take them on? Do we know the right words to say to the Devil, to evil by any other name?

Idea of the Day

Lord, you know the deepest wrestling in my soul right now. Give me the perseverance necessary to get beyond this devil [of doubt, loneliness, anxiety, anger, judgmentalism, pride, addiction].

Abide

For forty wilderness days and nights he was tested by Satan.
Wild animals were his companions, and angels took care of him.

Mark 1:13

Animals and angels! That's quite a pairing. Only in Mark's temptation story do we hear about Jesus having such a lot of interesting company after his exhausting ordeal. Matthew, who borrowed Mark's story, holds onto the angels but dumps the beasts. Luke, who normally adds in angels at every opportunity, prefers to portray Jesus as conspicuously deprived of either species in his version of this event.

Mark, for his part, offers few details of the epic struggle. We never hear from Mark what Satan offers or how Jesus replies. Sin is sin, after all, tedious and pedestrian. We know how it goes without having it all spelled out for us. Satisfaction, power, money, fame. The channels of temptation haven't changed much over the millennia.

But afterwards: the wild animals and the angels? Creatures of earth and heaven surround Jesus, providing a cosmic hug of reassurance at the end. Jesus succeeds in the way Adam and Eve once failed. He says yes to God and no to serving any other authority. Consequently, Jesus enjoys the peaceable kingdom Isaiah once talked about, the New Eden in which fierce beasts are tamed and the threat of the wild is overcome. Nature is no longer oppositional to its own. The violence of the world runs dry as original sin loses its grip.

Of course, we know this story too well not to remember that violence will overtake Jesus in just a few short years. There will come an hour when the angels must surrender him, and the beasts will be human and turn quite cruel. This portrait of the triumph of Jesus in the wild remains revelatory. We too are poised between the forces of heaven and those of earth, threatened by beasts and guarded by angels. We live in harmony when we honor God and refuse to obey an imperfect authority. Like our own, for example. All can go dark and dangerous in a heartbeat when we bow to the Liar instead.

Idea of the Day

Where do I see the beasts of violence on the outside? How much violence resides in me, and what circumstances bring it out of hiding?

First Sunday of Lent (Year C)

Trust

Jesus answered by quoting Deuteronomy:
"It takes more than bread to really live." **Luke 4:4**

Desert is a word that lends no comfort. It conveys barrenness, absence, a lack of some sort: "This place is deserted!" or "It was a real desert experience for me."

So when Jesus begins his mission by retreating into desert wilderness, this is an ascetic choice. He withdraws from all human resources and trusts his fate to God. That's part of it, anyway. The other part is the hate/hate relationship Israelites had with the desert. They'd once spent forty years staggering around in one, waiting for Moses to lead them across a stretch of ground that, as the crow flies, might have taken two weeks. It wasn't that Moses was lousy with directions. Since the Israelites had proven unfit for their new role as the free children of God after the slavery years in Egypt, Moses was forced to wait until that whole generation died off before he could proceed.

Since that time, the desert has been seen as the ultimate spiritual proving ground. It is the terrain where the devil stares you in the face and you have to learn to stand firm. If you want to be truly free, you have to learn to resist enslavement to the forces of darkness. The symbolic forty days Jesus spends in the desert represents those forty lost years, and, in his victory, Jesus redeems them.

What we glean from these stories is that the desert is not an empty place at all. It's inhabited by our own worst self, taunting us to surrender to it. This is why our first Sunday contemplation of Lent concerns the wilderness landscape. It's here that our needs catch up with us, and our fears assail us. We need bread and water just to survive. But to do more than survive, to truly live, that won't be enough.

During Lent, we don't fast for forty days as Jesus did. But we are trying to recapture something of that desert experience in our observance of this season. We hope to rediscover what's essential, what the bread of our existence is. We need to know where the demons are and what they want from us. We need to test our interior resources, and, most of all, we must know where they end and our reliance on God's grace must begin.

Idea of the Day

How do my chosen lenten practices re-create the desert landscape with its valuable proving ground?

Prioritize

The revelation of GOD is whole and pulls our lives together.
The signposts of GOD are clear and point out the right road.

Psalm 19:7–8

Normally I don't look for life lessons from Capitol Hill. But recently a politician wrote that government should identify its top three priorities. If we don't know what they are, he suggested, we don't have priorities. It occurs to me that this is not only true, it's also dangerous. When you and I live without priorities—or, to use the religious term, values—it's an invitation to drift. We may wake up in the middle of our lives or at the end of them and realize our lives have been about nothing at all.

Identifying our values shouldn't be a guessing game. It ought to be clear to us (and even more transparent to others) what our lives are about. Each of us might express our top three values with different words: Love, generosity, peace. Kindness, reverence, joy. Gratefulness, holiness, courage. Humility, gentleness, truth. In whatever combination we choose, our values should represent gospel tradition and be signposts for our decision making and ground rules for our relationships.

We can look to the ten commandments to identify values like obedience, honor, fidelity, and honesty. The teaching Jesus offers about what separates sheep from goats gives us more to choose from: charity, compassion, presence, justice. The beatitudes also define what our lives should be about: mercy, righteousness, purity. We might choose three values now and post them during these forty days as a reminder of the direction in which we hope to conform our lives. Don't worry if you change your mind later: you can always add to the list. There's no such thing as harboring too many values!

I secretly believe that any one of the gospel values, if followed conscientiously, will lead us to the rest of them. Think of them as avenues culminating in the same town square. But it's also helpful to remember Saint Paul's words: "And regardless of what else you put on, wear love. It's your basic, all-purpose garment. Never be without it" (Col. 3:14).

Idea of the Day

Brainstorm the values that have shaped your life the most so far. Then ask yourself: are these the central values I want to carry into the future? Is this who I really want to be?

First Week of Lent: Tuesday

Submit

You're in charge!
You can do anything you want!
You're ablaze in beauty!
Yes. Yes. Yes.

MATTHEW 6:13

AMEN IS A WORD WE MOSTLY GET WRONG. We put it at the
end of our prayers dully, like a period. The "Yes. Yes. Yes." of *The
Message* gets closer to the heart of this Hebrew word. Amen is
our response to the whole of the prayer, our affirmation of what's
been said, the seal of our witness to the event of prayer itself.

There's a lot going on in The Lord's Prayer, of which the verse above is a part, and we want to be alert to all of it before signing on the dotted line with our amen. With this prayer, we're inviting God into our daily dealings. We're asking for the kingdom to be revealed to us—hold on, do we really want this? Are we prepared to receive the kingdom and respond to it? We're embracing the mutuality of mercy: we get it to the measure that we give it. We also make petition for stuff we need: food, and grace under trial.

Most of us are glad to make petition for our needs, but otherwise we'd prefer that heaven stay out of our business. A close inspection of our daily decisions by the Power That Is wouldn't do us any favors. We snap at people, take the best piece of pie, ignore suffering that requires our response, and hold others bound by our unforgiveness. A simple reflection on my choices so far today isn't very promising for my future canonization. The bottom line is I still want to have things my own way.

The Lord's Prayer is finally a prayer of submission—an ugly word to freedom-loving folks like us. Yet as soon as we agree to call God "Our Father," submission isn't far behind. Dare I suggest that it's not our liberty that's at risk here, but rather our rugged individualism and independence? Once we call God "Father," we embrace membership in the family of faith. Once we belong to family, we exchange independence for interdependence. There's no "me" anymore, just "us." There's no more "my way," either, as we surrender our will to a far better one.

Idea of the Day

Adopt this simple prayer and repeat it throughout the day: "You're in charge." Surrender to new and wonderful possibilities by making God's will your own!

Repent

Everyone must turn around, turn back from an evil life...
Who knows? Maybe God will turn around
and change his mind about us!

JONAH 3:8–9

HAVE YOU EVER HAD TO REINVENT YOURSELF? Changing schools or relocating with our parents in childhood gives us license to start again in a new context. Moving into the world solo is another big opportunity to try on a new identity. Marriage jettisons the solo act and embraces couplehood, then parenthood. A new place of employment or a new career may transform our sense of self entirely.

Other transformations are less welcome. Loss of a partner in death or divorce shatters our familiar identity and makes us nearly unrecognizable for a time. Illness or disability creates new boundaries to which we must adjust. Going to war, or to prison, or into a foreign land as a refugee, challenges the most solid identities with new information about what we're capable of. Even in a charmed life to which no exterior changes seem to intrude, the aging process will eventually reinvent us inside and out, like it or not.

Since change is inevitable, why not accept it, even actively direct it? To make room for the new, we must abandon some of the old, or at least prune the heck out of it. We might consider the lesson the Ninevites of Jonah's story learned: prune or be pruned! We don't have to wait for the warning either: "In forty days Nineveh will be smashed." We already know Nineveh is toast unless it repents. Which is to say, unless we do.

The church provides us with a checklist for the pruning process: name your sins, say you're sorry, ask for forgiveness, make restitution, resolve to do better. Children learn these steps to reconciliation in their playground squabbles; so they shouldn't seem alien to grownups. The sacrament enables us to do this ritually, just as the Ninevites don sackcloth and ashes to signal their communal change of heart. But in changing lanes, the signal is only the first step. After that, you really have to assume the new position.

Idea of the Day

Is there a lenten penance service coming up at which I can signal that I'm ready to change lanes? Are there partners in crime I should put on notice that I'm going to be someone new from now on?

Dare

Don't play hide and seek with us, O Lord.
It's time for you to reveal yourself.
Esther C25

Prayer isn't for sissies. In the Bible, when the heroes get down on their faces or up on their feet to pray, they gather all the *chutzpah* they can to tell God precisely what's on their minds. So Abraham once dickered with God over the fate of Sodom. So Moses climbed Mt. Sinai to meet his Maker and receive the Law. So the boy Solomon asked for wisdom to rule. So the prophets insisted God back up oracles with action. So widows accosted prophets and demanded they make good on their promises. In the gospels, the woman who grabs the hem of Jesus' clothes, the centurion who asks Jesus to order a healing without bothering to come under his roof, and the mother who begs Jesus to heal her non-Jewish daughter are all operating out of the same spiritual playbook. If you want something from God, don't beat around the bush. Say what you mean and go for it!

The three great female protagonists of the Old Testament— Ruth, Judith, and Esther—are all drawn as women desperate and determined enough to seize the day in very unladylike ways. This makes for wonderful drama as Ruth secures a husband and future, Judith vanquishes an enemy, and Esther saves a nation: all in a day's work for these holy women! It's not just about the drama, or these books wouldn't be in the Bible. It's about whole-souled confidence in God, the kind that speaks and acts fearlessly.

By contrast, a lot of the praying we do in church is pretty tepid, truth be told. The words are pious and flowery. They're doctrinally correct but technical and passionless. They sound like they were written by a committee, and some of them are. It's as if we're secretly afraid to ask for too much or to expect anything at all from God. It's easier to hide behind formulas that dilute our intercessions down to nothing much. Do we think God doesn't care, or that no one's really listening?

Idea of the Day
Pray like a biblical hero. Tell God what's going on, how you feel, what you need. Be encouraged by the example of Jesus, who asked forgiveness for his enemies, wondered if God had abandoned him, and still surrendered his spirit to God in the end.

Think

Carelessly call a brother 'idiot!' and you just might
find yourself hauled into court.
Thoughtlessly yell 'stupid!' at a sister
and you are on the brink of hellfire.
The simple moral fact is that words kill.

MATTHEW 5:22

WORDS HAVE POWER. A nineteenth-century playwright once declared the pen mightier than the sword. While pens, swords, and professional writers seem so last-century now, words remain vitally significant.

Think about how a phrase can define reality. Children who

are told they're worthless are devalued in their own eyes. Words like fat, ugly, lazy, or stupid hurt us in the classroom and still hurt now, decades after they were spoken. In the same way, encouragement and kindness also shape our early egos and make us capable of greater things. Not the least of which is offering good words to the next person who needs them.

"I love you" has quite an impact on our lives. So does "Go away" or "I don't need you." We can convey most information gently or harshly. The only reason to be rough is to register annoyance and put someone down. Is that what we intend? If we think before we speak, would we choose our words more carefully?

Speech is mercurial. It slips out and betrays our intentions before we know we intend anything at all. How many cutting phrases might we take back if only we could! How many foolish remarks have cost us alliances, friendships, marriages, or contented relationships with children and grandchildren!

Compare careless words with divinely purposeful ones. God creates the world with words: "Let there be light"—and there is. Is it possible to redeem the work of words to be creative and productive, rather than weapons of mass destruction? Yes. We can think before we speak, type, text, or hit the Send key. It may feel good for a moment to tell that jerk who cut us off in traffic precisely where we think he ought to spend eternity. Considering the authority in words, we'll get more bang from a blessing than a curse.

Idea for the Day

I'll spend one day choosing my words thoughtfully. Will that make me quieter than usual? I offer my abstinence today for those I've wounded with words.

Mature

In a word, what I'm saying is, Grow up.
You're kingdom subjects. Now live like it. MATTHEW 5:48

MY OLD PARISH HAD AN ONGOING PROGRAM CALLED "GROWING IN FAITH." GIF for short. We GIF-ers met once a month to attend a presentation about some aspect of church teaching, history, theology, liturgy, or spirituality. Then we'd discuss it. Finally, we'd decide what we felt called to do in response to it.

The most commonly uttered sentence during GIF night discussions was: "I never knew that!" Granted, some of our members were returning Catholics who'd been away from the church for a while. They'd joined the group in hopes of coming up to speed on matters of faith. But others were lifer Catholics, faithful in their attendance for fifty, sixty, seventy years. If being Catholic is measured by reception of the sacraments and supporting the parish financially, these folks were stellar examples.

Yet some of these good people were fuzzy on anything that happened in the Old Testament after Noah's ark or the time of Moses. The contribution of Saint Paul seemed vague and unappealing. Some had no idea that the color of vestments the priest wore each Sunday was not Father's personal fashion statement, but an indication of the season the church was celebrating. The Reformation, the Council of Trent, and even Vatican Council II were terms of uncertain significance. Most attendees embraced an emphatic pro-life position—until they understood that the consequences were much wider than protecting the life of the unborn. After the first year of meetings, we all admitted some confusion in separating church teaching from sources like hearsay, cultural norms, patriotism, and personal family practices. Practicing religion long but not deep wasn't working.

We learned from all this what may be a troublesome truth: church isn't simply about going to church. We are not the church so that we can go to church. Jesus founded the church for a mission: to go forth, as we say at Mass. We must learn here those things that have ramifications out there. If we're church for ourselves, to save our souls, we've got it all wrong. We're church for the sake of those who are not church. It's a compelling idea.

Idea of the Day

How deep is my understanding of my faith? What aspects are particularly shallow or uncertain? What can I do to mature in understanding?

Shine

While [Peter] was going on like this, babbling,
a light-radiant cloud enveloped them,
and sounding from deep in the cloud a voice:
"This is my Son, marked by my love, focus of my delight.
Listen to him." **MATTHEW 17:5**

WHO DELIGHTS YOU? Whom do you delight? In various seasons of life, we probably answer these questions differently. As Ecclesiastes says, there's a time for all sorts of things! In youth, our delight is in romantic ideals of love: the boyfriend, the bride, the unrequited passion of a celebrity poster in a dorm room. Later, our delight may be in the long-familiar face of a spouse,

favorite sister, or friend we've known since grammar school. The face of delight may belong to a child or grandchildren. If you're a mystic, the face of delight may be the beatific vision of God, the Madonna, or the saints who chat with you in privileged communion.

While Peter babbles about clinging to the privileged encounters on Transfiguration mountain, he nearly misses the main event. While he and James and John are transfixed by the revealed glory of a friend they thought they knew, heaven is also gazing at that same face. Heaven knows Jesus as he always is, and that celestial view is momentarily shared with these three bewildered friends.

The love of God marks the one who receives and acknowledges it. Being the focus of God's delight *and knowing it* makes every saint radiant—which is where the idea of the halo comes from. It's why Moses came down from Sinai with a face so shiny he had to wear a veil. It's why Our Lady of Guadalupe wears a full-body halo: blessed among women, Mary gave herself up body and soul to be God's delight. When you know you're the recipient of God's love, it's impossible to hide it.

When you meet a real live saint—and there are some, walking around right now in places you may not expect—you'll know him or her by the glow. When you and I accept that we are also God's great delight, marked by that same love, we'll shine too.

Idea of the Day

Lord, is it true? Do you really love me that much? I'm surprised. I want to ask why. Because you know me better than anyone. But you also know who I can become, with enough time and grace.

Savor

Peter interrupted, "Rabbi, this is a great moment!
Let's build three memorials—one for you, one for Moses,
one for Elijah." He blurted this out without thinking.

MARK 9:5–6A

I THINK WE LOVE PETER IN THE GOSPEL STORIES BECAUSE HE REPRESENTS US, THE CHURCH. His reactions are our reactions. He says what the rest of us are thinking. If my pastor suddenly radiated light and sprouted prophets, I'd want to enshrine the moment too! This kind of thing doesn't happen every day. Writer Marcel Proust coined the term "privileged moments" to describe events through which we seem to see, as in a dim mirror, the higher, clearer realities hidden in the present. Most family Bibles let us know quite plainly what the privileged moments are, consigning them to full-color plates. Stained-glass church windows are also "shout-outs" of events that literally became windows on cosmic truth breaking into mundane history.

Like Peter, our impulse is to savor these moments. Recall a time when you looked around and realized: this is an hour that won't come again; this is a happening with life-changing significance. Your heart becomes a camera, your mind a biographer, creating a record of the event to last a lifetime.

I used to visit a nursing home where a translucent soul resided. Mrs. Luce was 103 when I knew her: her name actually means light. Her darling husband was long gone, her children too, all her friends lost to the miles, to the years, to death. She was bedridden, hearing going, and fairly blind. Each time I visited we had to start over, since memory no longer served such a late-coming acquaintance.

But oh, the privileged moments of her life were intact! She'd been a young woman at the time of the 1906 San Francisco earthquake. She had gone into the city to get her wedding dress: alas, the city was on fire! But then her soon-to-be husband came after her in his fine carriage. He swooped down and caught her by the waist, lifting her into the carriage. And in his arms, at that moment, she knew everything would be all right. Each time she told this story, the young girl of 1906 would shine free from her wrinkled face, and I saw her. I knew the girl every bit as well as I did the old dying woman before me.

Idea of the Day

What are my privileged moments, upon which my life story is based? What do they teach me about love, and hope?

Emerge

They turned out to be Moses and Elijah—and what a glorious appearance they made! They talked over his exodus, the one Jesus was about to complete in Jerusalem. **LUKE 9:30–31**

THE ROAD OUT. That's what exodus means. The big exodus in the Old Testament is the one that leads out of slavery in Egypt. It's what the book called Exodus is all about, even though the escape happens in the first third of the story. Getting physically out of Egypt is one thing. Getting Egypt out of your head is another. Slave mentality is hard to get beyond. Freedom isn't free to the one who still lives in fear, beaten down and dependent.

In the end, the only way to leave Egypt behind was to leave

the generation that once knew slavery behind too. Not one Israelite adult who lived in Egypt crossed over the Jordan into the Promised Land. Not even Moses, who only gets to view Canaan from the top of Mt. Nebo. Then he relinquishes control to Joshua, who'd been a boy at the time of the great escape. Children are more flexible, adaptable. Grownups find it really tough to change their minds, their hearts, and their ways.

Exodus, the road out, is a metaphor for death. The only way out of one existence and into another is through death. We all know this, because we've died many times. We've died to dreams we had, things we tried and failed to do. We've died in loves that were betrayed, in hearts broken. We've died to convictions we were so sure of (that's what convictions are!) only to find out we couldn't be more wrong. We've died to our shining illusions of who we are: better, nobler, smarter, stronger than everyone around us. We've died to the stubborn fantasy that life is all about us, our goals, our wishes, and our wills.

When Jesus confers with the two ancient representatives of law and prophecy, they appreciate the path he's on. They know the road to Jerusalem is humanity's ultimate exodus from the consequences of sin and death. Jesus is going down that road. He's going to free the slaves of history, open the door of death, and walk right through it.

Idea of the Day

Lord, how free am I? Am I held by chains of unresolved anger, regret, anxiety, injury, addiction? Help me die to this slavery and to be born again a free child of God.

Confess

Oh yes, GOD, we've been exposed in our shame, all of us—
our kings, leaders, parents—before the whole world.
And deservedly so, because of our sin. **Daniel 9:7–8**

Scandal is great for business, if the business you're in is selling media. But it's not great for much else. Derived from the Greek word *skandalon*, meaning stumbling block, a scandal trips people up. It makes powerful people fall down on their faces, which we don't mind so much. There's a German word for why we don't mind: *schadenfreude*, which literally means "damage-joy" and roughly translates as "I love it when you suffer."

"Damage-joy" is just one reason why scandals are bad. They bring out the worst in everyone. They demonstrate that the mighty are vulnerable, which causes malicious glee in those who feel powerless. Scandals reveal that so-called holy people are capable of behaving incredibly badly. This gives the rest of us a veneer of license to go on being lazy about our own virtue. Scandals make leaders look foolish, and turn heroes into hypocrites. This makes the person on the street a tad more reluctant to invest confidence in any leadership, and it makes us all a bit more cynical about the mirage of goodness.

In these ways, scandals hurt all of us, those exposed and shamed as well as those who do the exposing and shaming. In our generation, relentless scandals have caused a tremendous loss of confidence in church and government: ANY church, ANY government. The alarming number of children being raised without the firm foundation of their parents' marriage beneath them has also led to a scandal in the reliability of marriage itself: what does marriage mean as an institution of society if it can be dispensed with so easily or never engaged to begin with?

One big problem with scandal these days is that there is so darn much of it—perhaps not more than any other time in history, but we know about it now, every tiny thread of it. Nothing escapes the camera phone, the tweet, the blog, the six o'clock news report. We know more about the inner souls of strangers than we ever want to know. All of which, oddly enough, masks our own culpability. We no longer say: "There but for the grace of God, go I." Now we say: "Better him than me."

Idea of the Day

Do I indulge in "damage-joy"? Am I becoming more cynical? Have I lost faith in leadership as a construct? Do I believe all institutions are corrupt?

Purify

Go home and wash up.
Clean up your act.
ISAIAH 1:16

HYGIENE IS IMPORTANT. I'm reminded of this each time I see my dentist. If I've done a good job the last six months, I get a pat on the head and a fresh toothbrush. If I've been less keen on flossing, however, I get another appointment, a world of pain, and a big bill in my future. At the end of the ordeal, I ask myself: really, how hard is it to floss regularly?

Spiritual hygiene isn't much different. We know the rules. We know what thou shalt not do, and what thou really ought to be doing. We know about sin and grace, and we're pretty sure which is which as we review our options. Every trusted spiritual authority assures us that praying daily is a good thing and that receiving the sacraments often is a great help. We have Scriptures to enlighten us, church teaching to guide us, parish life to companion us, study groups to challenge us, service projects to expand us, and the great yawning need of the world to summon us. What more do we need to get our act together?

We don't want for information. What's often lacking is simple dedication to the care and maintenance of our eternal lives. Eternity, remember, doesn't start after we die. We're swimming in it now. Eternity isn't a future maybe; it's a present reality. Too often the tangibility of "real life" takes priority over the spooky-misty ambiguity of pie-in-the-sky-when-we-die. If eternity meant future pie and I had to choose between that and the pie on the plate in front of me, my fork would already be in the plate.

But if eternity includes now, it includes today's pie on today's plate. Eternity includes what I do with my love in this hour: whether I want to be with God right now as well as forever. Am I on God's side, am I a friend of the good? Is religion a game I play to keep up the appearance of decency? Do I want and intend to become the person I was created to be? Or am I prepared to accept a world of pain now, and a big bill in the future?

Idea of the Day

What's my spiritual routine and how serious am I about practicing it? Is there more I could be doing to improve the health of my immortal life?

Drink

And [Jesus] said to James and John,
"Are you capable of drinking the cup that I'm about to drink?"
They said, "Sure, why not?"
Jesus said, "Come to think of it, you are going to drink my cup.
But as to awarding places of honor, that's not my business."

MATTHEW 20:22B–23

WE'RE ALL IN THIS TOGETHER. The business of church, that
is. From baptism on we've elected to be the Body of Christ on
earth. We're drinking from the same cup: old and young, rich
and poor, folks of every race and language, newcomer and lifer
Catholic, educated and illiterate, gifted and challenged alike.

The atmosphere of a given parish may not reflect this reality of our holy communion. We may glare at each other across the aisles. We may wish the young people would dress more appropriately for Mass. Or that the old ladies obstructing the view of the sanctuary with their hats would get over their fussy traditionalism. A Spanish verse added to a hymn at the English Mass makes temperatures rise. A foreign-born priest assigned to the parish causes offense. We're tired of second collections for distant needs. We dread when RCIA rituals are assigned to our Mass, throwing off our timing on Sunday morning. We're uncomfortable with homeless people loitering on the premises, here to escape the elements and clearly not to worship.

We drink from the cup of a common humanity, sharing an identity as God's children. But we also drink from the same cup as Jesus did, which means something more. It means we're all going to suffer in this world, and we're all going to die. My suffering is not the same as that of the toothless man with the unwashed hair and ratty clothes sleeping in the last pew. But because I do suffer, he and I are kin in the realm of pain and need.

How quickly James and John agree to drink from the cup of Jesus! How blithely do we often approach the sacrament, eating and drinking without weighing the significance of this contract carved out in flesh and blood. If we don't intend communion with Christ and each other, taking communion becomes a dangerous self-deception.

Idea of the Day

Are there groups within my community from whom I am estranged or disapproving? What step might I take to promote real communion with them?

Examine

"But I, GOD, search the heart and examine the mind.
I get to the heart of the human. I get to the root of things.
I treat them as they really are, not as they pretend to be."
JEREMIAH 17:10

**THE EXAMINATION OF CONSCIENCE CAN SOUND A BIT
OLD-SCHOOL FOR SOME OF US WHO HAVEN'T DARKENED
THE DOOR OF A CONFESSIONAL IN A WHILE.** It's not a practice immediately linked to sacramental action—although it may
bring us to that hour sooner or later. Reflecting on the day and
its harvest of good and rotten fruit is something most of us wind
up doing anyway—often at midnight as we relive a happy victory

or gnaw on an unresolved argument.

So why not consecrate the habit to better purposes? The examination of conscience can be formal: a review of preprinted questions about our actions and intentions kept at bedside or near a chosen "prayer chair." It can be digital: a quick log of "Cheers/Regrets" for the week. Journal writers may find a "P.S. Examen" at day's end to be helpful. Writing things down has the added advantage of presenting us with a map of where we're headed. Did we really lose our temper every day this week? Has despair become so habitual? Are we having conflicts at work less frequently this month? What's going on that we swear now more than ever? Are we moving from fear to action more quickly? Has generosity become our default response to that needy family member at last?

Daily recollection is a wonderfully private affair, so we can be very frank with ourselves and with God (who knows us through and through anyway). There's no reason to tell less than the whole truth: the good, the bad, the ugly. Where the trust level is high enough and faith is mutual, we may also choose to recollect regularly with a spouse, as a family, or within our religious community. This isn't a time to "rat on each other," but to practice honesty and transparency. If religion remains a game of pretend, it will never get us far, and certainly not where we hope to go.

Idea of the Day

What method of self-evaluation works best for me? How often do I take the time to consider the patterns of my day and the habits I am forming?

Resist

Israel loved Joseph more than any of his other sons because he was the child of his old age. And he made him an elaborately embroidered coat. **GENESIS 37:3**

WE CALLED HER SAINT LUCILLE. My oldest sister could do no wrong in my father's eyes. A hard worker, surrendering her playtime at a moment's notice to do the most disagreeable chores, Lucille was the super-daughter, and upon her was heaped lavish and relentless praise. It could be suffocating for the rest of us—kids of average virtue and mediocre work ethic—to be compared unfavorably with our household saint at every turn. We wondered: did Lucille have to raise the bar so high, making the rest of us look so bad?

It can be argued that Jacob (AKA Israel) started the mess among his sons with parental favoritism and a fancy coat. Statistically, most parents of more than one child play favorites—and the favorite knows who she or he is. So do the non-favorites, who endure the legacy of also-ran for their parents' affections. To this day when I hear the saga of the Amazing Technicolor Dreamcoat and its injurious effect on all of Jacob's boys, I can't help but remember growing up in the shadow cast by my older sister's halo. It was hard on all of us. Even Lucille paid dearly for her early perfection.

Still, jealousy is a personal choice. None of us has to go there. Was Jacob to blame for doting on the child he'd longed to conceive with his beloved wife Rachel? Was Joseph to blame for being that son and enjoying the special attentions? The other brothers might have shrugged and found other ways to distinguish themselves. After all, they were older and it was time they got over their hunger for paternal approval. Instead, they capitalized on their sense of rejection, nursed the spirit of grievance, and focused on revenge fantasies. These choices brought them to the brink of murder.

It's been said these dastardly decisions led to the salvation of the family in the long run. But that's not quite true. God can bring good things out of the worst evil; it doesn't make evil desirable for a minute. If we're already in the ugly zone, God can rescue us even there. Better yet, we can resist going there in the first place.

Idea of the Day

Do I want what others have? What other choices are available to me in unjust situations besides brooding? My abstinence today reminds me to refrain from coveting what's not mine.

Celebrate

"[The houseboy] told him, 'Your brother came home.
Your father has ordered a feast—barbecued beef!—
because he has him home safe and sound.'" **LUKE 15:27**

WE SHOULDN'T HAVE TO SAY THIS IN CHURCH: THE BOTTOM LINE IN CHRISTIANITY IS CELEBRATION. The gospel is called good news for a reason! So where's the beef, we might ask? The barbecued beef, that is. Where's the spirit of celebration?

I once belonged to a parish in which the pastor never uttered a funny line or cracked a smile during the homily. This was unusual, because I knew the guy, and he had a great sense of humor. When I asked him why he was so stiff at the ambo, he admitted that the community he presently served didn't appreciate humor in church. It was true; I saw those grim faces every Sunday, hard as granite even at the Easter Vigil. These people took their religion seriously, by which they implied it was castor oil for the sick soul.

If a hymn was too happy, they didn't sing it. If a feast was too festive, they doubled down on morbidity. We sang dirges on Sundays during the Easter Season. It was as if the community feared the spirit of joy might sneak in and render their faith frivolous.

But you know, even Lent is no time to mourn. The root of the English word "Lent" means Spring. It's a time for blooming, not groaning. Purple is a penitential color, but repentance is a joyful thing, like the return of the lost son in the parable. "He's home!" is no cry of reproach, but one of amazement and gratitude. If we come back to God dragging our misery behind us like Marley's chains in *A Christmas Carol*, all the more reason to break out the barbecue.

There is such a thing as taking religion too seriously, by taking ourselves too seriously in the religious context. God isn't the Grim Reaper. No one ever died of smiling in church. If we've understood anything we've heard there so far, we have abundant reasons to be happy in church—and out of it. The party starts here!

Idea of the Day

Lord, is my faith something that makes me glad to be alive? If not, maybe I need to find a community that's grilling some good news.

Third Sunday of Lent (Year A)

Include

"How come you, a Jew, are asking me, a Samaritan woman, for a drink?" (Jews in those days wouldn't be caught dead talking to Samaritans.) **John 4:9**

I'm often impressed with how many new and creative ways I find to be a jerk in public. I was sitting with a woman I've known and admired for her great generosity. We were sharing a story about a man of our acquaintance, and I made a joke at the expense of his political party, to which I am not affiliated. My woman friend turned to me and said, "That's my party too, you know." I blanched. I mostly certainly did not know or even suspect. Immediately my mind started spinning.

Had I been wrong about this woman's merits during our acquaintance? If she had those sorts of alliances, surely she wasn't who I thought she was. Of course, she had an alliance with me as well, so what did that prove? Could I have been wrong about what sort of people "those people" are?

Prejudice never serves us well. There is simply no group of people we can safely hate, because it always turns out that we actually like some of them, believe it or not. We can't dismiss a whole gender, race, nationality, religion, orientation, political party, occupation, generation: name it, and with a little digging you'll find out one of your friends or family members is represented there. Or is about to marry someone who is. In my originally uniformly Catholic family, for example, we now host Protestants, Mormons, Muslims, and Jews at our family reunions, and they are all "us." The world is even smaller today than it was in the days that Jesus kept bumping into Samaritans. Somewhere in your family closet, you'll find a Samaritan hiding in plain view.

The woman at the well spelled out all the distinctions between herself and Jesus at a glance. He was a Jew, number one, reason enough to a Samaritan not to have this conversation. She was also a woman in a culture that frowned on easy exchanges with men who were not family members. Jesus obviously didn't belong here, since he'd come to a well without a bucket. This conversation should not have happened. But it did, and it changed everything.

Idea of the Day

Are there groups within my community to whom I never speak, who are not included on my list of acceptable people? Where might I begin to befriend a nearby "Samaritan"?

Protest

[Jesus] told the dove merchants, "Get your things out of here!
Stop turning my Father's house into a shopping mall!"

John 2:16

ANGER IS A CAPITAL SIN, FEATURED ON THE LIST OF SEVEN DEADLIES. *Caput* is Latin for head; therefore, capital sins represent seven occasions that are the most reliable trailheads down the road of error and misery. (For the record, the complete list of capital sins are: pride, anger, lust, envy, sloth, greed, and gluttony.) Since most of us have an acquaintance of some of these, and all of us bear a weakness for at least one, we've been down these trails far enough to agree: it's best not to entertain the near occasion of such behavior under normal circumstances.

Calling anger a potential road to disaster doesn't mean all anger is inappropriate. Some things should make us plenty mad, and that anger should motivate us to do more than vent our spleens in impotent rage. Jesus isn't portrayed as a rage-aholic in the gospels. But he does yell at religious leaders who are hypocrites, and he does cause a memorable scene in the Temple courtyard when commerce overwhelms a place that's supposed to be reserved for higher things.

Business at the Temple mount is connected to the ritual goings-on at the Temple itself. Profane money from all corners of the world needs to be exchanged for a purer currency for offering. Animals and grains need to be purchased on site since it's a whole lot easier than bringing the critters all the way from Cyrene or wherever the worshipper calls home. We appreciate, however, that the whole scene's gotten out of control. Making a profit has obscured the purpose of the hour. Religion, Inc. has turned the house of God into a franchise of Doves'R'Us. Jesus registers his offense.

Jesus is likewise offended at the sight of poor souls whose natural liberty is eclipsed by their demons: daughters of Abraham who need healing and the self-righteous folk who would deny it to them because it's a holy day; sinners who need the medicine of religion and who are kept from it precisely because they are sinners; disciples who should know better than to seek greatness for themselves and security for Jesus. When something's wrong, get angry about it. Then seek the means to make it right.

Idea of the Day

God in heaven, if there's suffering around here that I can do something about, show me how. If it's time for me to speak up about injustice, give me the courage.

Imagine

*These are all warning markers—DANGER!—in our history
books, written down so that we don't repeat their mistakes...
We are just as capable of messing it up as they were.*
1 CORINTHIANS 10:11–12

**HISTORY IS OFTEN PRESENTED AS THE STORY OF HUMAN
ACHIEVEMENTS.** But it's just as fair to view it as a litany of
human failures. Elementary school textbooks review the past
as a succession of empires, invasions, wars, and conquests. Our
fixation on conflict as *the* story led one historian to define "the
end of history" as a time when the great tensions between East
and West are finally resolved.

How messed up is that? Is a world at peace equivalent to the demise of progress and adventure? Is dominance and brutal competition the only way we know how to proceed?

Since biblical times we've told our story as a long wrestling match: man against woman, brother against brother, nation against nation. Scripture is ultimately presented as humanity rebelling against God. In the movie industry and the news media, two people yelling at each other—if not squaring off with guns—is the inevitable climactic scene. The result is polarity wherever you look: in our political process, our church, our neighborhoods, and our families.

It doesn't have to be this way. The prophetic vision of a peaceable kingdom (see Isaiah chapter 11), with wild beasts living in harmony and the child safely touching the serpent, is a revisiting of the Eden story with a happier ending. That future is presented not as a prediction but a possibility. We have to reach for it, work for it, and bring it to birth through the unswerving dedication to justice. But first of all, we have to believe in it.

If that seems too much trouble, then here's a guarantee: human history will be more of the same. Children of Abraham will continue to go down into slavery in places like Pharaoh's Egypt, and ambition-mad governors like Pilate will continue to slaughter helpless Galileans. We'll see a World War III, more terrorism and senseless violence, more people yelling and waving guns. What kind of future do we want?

Idea of the Day

New rules: from now on, I am going to be a peacemaker and avoid generating and participating in conflict.

Yearn

A white-tailed deer drinks from the creek;
I want to drink God, deep draughts of God.

PSALM 42:1–2

IF YOU WANT TO UNDERSTAND SOMETHING PROFOUND ABOUT GOD, FOLLOW THE WATER. From end to end the Bible is a story of water. It begins with the dark abyss, a place of chaos God determines to subdue and organize. From these dangerous depths God forms land and sky, separates waters above from those below, fills the seas with swimming things, the earth with creeping things, and the sky with flying things. And that's all in the first week.

Chaos returns in the flood story, and God dries up the land again—promising it won't happen a third time and providing us with rainbow insurance. Thereafter, God is the ready custodian of seas and rivers parted at convenient hours, the bringer of rains, the gatekeeper of the forces inherent in water. Waters heal, as in the story of Naaman the leper-general, or at the pools of Bethesda, or in the merest spittle of Jesus. No wonder John the Baptist resorts to the river Jordan to get his message across, just as Isaiah did eight centuries earlier: wash yourselves clean!

Jesus inherits his Father's authority over water, demonstrated in his uncanny ability to fill nets with fish, calm storms, and walk on the surface of the sea. Since the water that heals is the same water that potentially destroys, it has to be governed with a firm hand. The dual moods of water are expressed in our sacramental use of it: water breaks the chains of sin and supplies us with liberating new life.

Water quenches thirst. It soaks the soil and coaxes the seed into transformation. It cleans, purifies, refreshes, and delights us, body and soul. It makes the difference between a barren globe of rock and Planet Earth. Water is life.

So when the psalmist seeks God thirstily, this is no casual metaphor. The instinctive path of the deer to the creek teaches us about our own yearning. When we know what the deer knows—when we yearn for God like water—on that day we begin to live.

Idea of the Day

Dear God, what do I need to do to nurture my longing for your company? Is it time for a retreat, spiritual direction, or a complete change of heart?

Gamble

Don't ever, we beg you, abandon us—you have promised us otherwise, so please don't water down your covenant. Don't pry your mercy from our grasp. **DANIEL 3:34–35A**

THE BIGGEST GAMBLE OF OUR LIVES DOESN'T HAPPEN IN A CASINO, AT THE MOMENT OF A MARRIAGE PROPOSAL, OR WHEN WE SIGN ON THE DOTTED LINE AT THE REALTOR'S. As consequential as any of those occasions may be, the biggest gamble is taking up Pascal's Wager and deciding for or against God. Philosopher Blaise Pascal put it this way: if you trust in God and you're mistaken, you'll live a pretty good life and enjoy the admiration of others. And you won't know you were wrong until you're dead. You won't know anything, in fact. Whereas if you don't trust in God and you're mistaken, you spend eternity regretting the decision. Hence it's better to wager on God.

Most believers would call that a bland reason to head for the baptismal font, synagogue, mosque, or ashram. But it's good for starters if it motivates you to cross the threshold of faith. Honestly, during ten years working with the RCIA crowd, I heard all kinds of unusual reasons why people want to join the church: dreams and signs, childhood memories, grandmothers wielding rosaries, random moments in front of a candle stand, terminal illnesses, unexpected pregnancies, not to mention the faith of a fiancé, spouse, or friend. A few years of ministry with returning Catholics produced a similar list of reasons why people come back to church after a long absence: a new marriage, the death of a spouse, the birth of a child, sickness, healing, passages of every kind.

What this teaches me is that there are no bad reasons to approach the church or to get back in touch with the God quest, by any other name. We may use different doors but we're heading into the same Presence. People often describe the decision to gamble on God this way: "I don't know what it means, I don't know where this will lead…" That's true for all of us—cradle Catholics as well as those just testing the waters of faith. Discipleship is often a mystery tour, but there's no mystery at all about the outcome. If we gamble on God, our final destination is mercy.

Idea of the Week

How much do I have on the table when it comes to faith?
Am I playing for pennies or for keeps?

Focus

*Just make sure you stay alert. Keep close watch over yourselves.
Don't forget anything of what you've seen. Don't let your heart
wander off.* **DEUTERONOMY 4:9A**

**ATTENTION DEFICIT DISORDER IS RAMPANT IN A SOCI-
ETY AS DISTRACTIBLE AS OURS.** There's so much to see and
do and absorb and remember! We're entertained to death, in-
formed to within an inch of our lives, educated and overextended
in all directions. We may be exhausted, yet can't sleep because
our minds struggle at night to keep all of the daytime balls in the
air. Before vacations we work twice as hard to catch up before we
leave, and after we return; this makes us too worn out to enjoy

ourselves while we're away.

This is the brave new world. Short of hightailing it to a cloister, there's little chance of escaping it. But we can simplify, thereby saving our sanity for the things that require it. Here's a rule that cuts sorrow in half: *If you don't need to own something, don't.* Ownership is a two-edged sword because our possessions possess us right back. It's not just the purchase price, insurance, and upkeep that gets us. It's the time spent and the personal resources engaged that are the real killers. Houses and property, cars and boats and motorcycles and airplanes, gadgets and computers and televisions in every room are all royal time-sucks. Do we want to give our love and attention to people or to things?

The acronym FOMO says it all: many of us harbor a *Fear of Missing Out*. FOMO describes the anxiety that springs from being deprived of text messages, e-mail, or Facebook page for too long. I'm for OTMO: *Opt To Miss Out!* We don't have to be in the loop for every conversation and news cycle, all that's trending through. Consider how you can always skip a soap opera for two weeks and not miss a thing. Anything that "trends" while our backs are turned wasn't worth knowing about.

Finally: "Just Say No" is a good motto for more than addictive substances. We can say no to joining a new committee, missing another family dinner, drinking and eating irresponsibly, spending another evening mainlining media entertainment. Silence really is golden sometimes. So is solitude.

Idea of the Week

Is my life hectic? Do I need to slow down and simplify? What can I stop doing today?

Commit

"This is war, and there is no neutral ground.
If you're not on my side, you're the enemy; if you're not helping,
you're making things worse." **LUKE 11:23**

"MODERATION IN ALL THINGS" IS A PLEASING CATCH-
PHRASE. It comes from Aristotle, and was intended to recom-
mend a third route between excess and deficiency of action.
Saint Paul, a Greco-Roman sort of guy, seems to echo this value
whenever he counsels for temperance, or self-discipline. Don't
go overboard, and don't lose control. Keep to the serene middle
of the road. The bottom line seems to be: don't be an extremist.

Yet in Luke's gospel more than most, Jesus sounds exactly like

an extremist. You know what I mean: give away all your possessions; love your enemies; hate your parents; if you're not with me,
you're against me! Seriously, there's nothing moderate about the
gospel in Lucan terms. The rhetoric is wild, the terms unyielding.
If we met this Jesus in the streets today, many of us would cross
to the other side to avoid him.

Luke wrote his gospel in the 80s. I mean the real 80s.
Jerusalem was toast after 70 AD when the Romans destroyed
the Temple and scattered the leadership. Judaism collapsed at
the center and required a new, tighter self-definition. This ended
the tendency within Judaism to agree-to-disagree with followers of Jesus. After the Temple's destruction, you had to make a
choice between being a Jew or a Christian, between synagogue
or house church. No more compromising! In the same generation, attitudes heated up in the Empire toward both Judaism and
Christianity. To the Romans, there was no distinction between
these Palestinian religions. When Jews were expelled from Rome
in 49 AD, Christians had to leave too.

Nero began the active persecution of Christians in 64-68, a
purge which probably led to the deaths of Peter and Paul and
countless others. Appreciate the tenor of the times in which
Luke penned his account: this really was a war, and "Christian
soldiers" were dying in it! Forcing the hour of decision for believers became part of that. Wafflers, dabblers, and dilettantes
need not apply.

Idea of the Day

*Am I a spiritual dilettante, or a committed Christian? Does
my faith cost me more than an hour a week and a buck in
the basket?*

Return

*Assyria won't save us; horses won't get us where we want to go.
We'll never again say "our god" to something we've made
or made up. You're our last hope.* **HOSEA 14:3**

LET'S BE HONEST. Straying from one's religion is as enduring a spiritual tradition as fidelity. Chances are some fellow producing cave paintings 10,000 years ago awoke one day wondering if the hunting spirits he depicted really existed. Doubt is the shadow cast by faith. If Mother Teresa, John of the Cross, and Teresa of Avila struggled through some spiritually dark times, you and I won't be spared.

Faith-rattling factors come from all directions: the inadequacies and incompetencies of human institutions of religion, for one. The flaws and hypocrisies in individual religious leaders, for another. Life, health, or relationship crises can trigger rage and refusal in us: *Non serviam. I will not serve.* So can shocking historical events that cast up in the air everything we believed about God, ourselves, and the laws governing the universe. Other reasons for departing from faith are more mundane: boredom, ignorance, moral inconsistencies in our behavior, greed, and the overall attraction of creature comforts.

Whatever sets us wandering from faith, the return route is always the same. Repentance means turning around. We can withdraw from the new alliance we've chased, including over-confidence in our own resources. Superpowers often seem like the horse to back: Assyria, Babylon, or Rome in biblical days, or the United States (for now). Yet all empires wind up as historical dig sites eventually. And speaking of horses: once they were the most powerful advantage in any war, short of elephants. But whose army puts its faith in horses today?

Idols, too, aren't the same as yesterday's brand. They're not carved from wood or stone these days. Instead, they seem to emerge from unlikely parts of New Jersey or Los Angeles, acting out our fascination with bling, random romance, and easy fame. The orientation of our hearts does matter. There are gods. And there is God.

Idea of the Day

God, I've been chasing some strange alliances lately. Security, attention, praise, creature comforts: do I really need these things more than I need you? Let my abstinence today represent my willingness to give up my extra gods.

Incarnate

I'm after love that lasts, not more religion.
I want you to know GOD, not go to more prayer meetings.

HOSEA 6:6

FOR THE PRESENT GENERATION, RELIGION'S BECOME A TAINTED WORD. It's fashionable to declare: "I'm spiritual, not religious"—as if religion is merely the disposable shell of something true and lovely that dwells inside. While the Latin roots of *religio* are uncertain, the term always denoted respect for the sacred. It may have derived from *re-lego*, "to consider again carefully," or *re-ligare*, "to reconnect."

Appreciating the deep meaning of a word is important, especially if you're determined to dispose of it. Today, religion is largely identified with its institutions. Our present mistrust of all things institutional is part of what motivates the rejection of the word. Religion is viewed suspiciously as ritualized worship and a legalized attitude toward people and their predicaments. In our hearts, many of us truly believe that God can't be all about saying formal prayers, standing here, bowing there, and the rigid condemnation of *so many* groups of people who don't measure up to the rules.

Jesus does have rather a lot to say about those Pharisees who are good with rules and not so good with people. When asked for a hierarchy of laws, Jesus insists love of God and neighbor come first. Jesus is clear about the definition of neighbor, too: the person of whom we least approve. Any religion that doesn't make the love command primary and view the "unacceptable" person as worthy of care may be a lot of things, but it's not Christianity.

I find many folks who identify as "spiritual" do share my respect of the sacred. They consider carefully what the summons of Life and Love, by any other name, obliges them to do. They seek deeper connection to the Holy, to the wholeness of creation. If we lob the "pagan" grenade at genuine seekers and dismiss their strides toward integrity as worthless, we miss the path of dialogue that's an invitation to more.

We might consider our own integrity a little more too. How well do we incarnate what we profess?

Idea of the Day

Lord, in the spirit of true religion, help me to reconnect to you, and to the holiness and wholeness at the center of reality.

Anticipate

*"Rabbi, who sinned: this man or his parents,
causing him to be born blind?"
Jesus said, "You're asking the wrong question.
You're looking for someone to blame. There is no such cause-effect
here. Look instead for what God can do."* **JOHN 9:2–3**

IT'S HARD NOT TO DO IT. Not to ask, "Why me? What did I do to deserve this?" or "What did that old man do, or this little baby?" or " How could God let a tornado kill all those innocent people?"

Evil and suffering are twin monster mysteries to which no philosophy satisfactorily responds. Religious systems only describe

the monsters and aim to give their backstory, ranging from the whim of the gods to human arrogance. The only answer to evil and suffering that would suffice for us is one that makes them both go away, that repeals their effect and rids us of their disastrous consequences.

We want a world without cancer, a life beyond terror, a home free from natural disaster, a place where life doesn't hurt. If there ever was such an Eden, it's not recorded past the opening of Genesis. What we've got is this world, with all its warts and dangers and dreads. We live in a universe subject to rules we know about and some we don't. We're free choosers living among other choosers who sometimes choose the wrong. We're each given a body that is also a time bomb, and someday it will certainly go off. If we entertain any other fantasy about the human predicament, we're going to be disappointed.

And yet: that's not the whole story, for people of faith. Beyond limitations that chaff and burn, we also experience the call to transcendence. The saddest child facing the fewest options feels the same urgency toward a finer, better reality as you and I do. The dying woman in the hospital senses it. The depressed hotel maid lifts her eyes from her work and knows it too. The soldier far from his family and country, and the undocumented worker harvesting strawberries for supermarkets he'll never visit, pins his hopes on it. All of us together look to what God can do, because we believe this much: when it comes to transcendence, God is the only one who delivers.

Idea of the Day

Which limiting conditions in my present circumstances must be accepted? Which can be transcended, and what can I do to participate in that movement?

Believe

This is how much God loved the world. He gave his Son, his one and only Son. And this is why: so that no one need be destroyed; by believing in him, anyone can have a whole and lasting life. JOHN 3:16

"NO CHILD LEFT BEHIND" HAS ALWAYS HAD A WONDERFUL RING TO IT. How it translates into politics is another matter. But how it translates into religion is pretty amazing. In God's eyes no one is worthless. No one is too poor, too sick, too wicked, too young or old to be beyond rescue. There are no spare people. There are no souls created for nothing. No life is destined to wind up on the cutting-room floor of history. No one is created by mistake.

Anyone can have a whole and lasting life! That's the divine plan.

Our plans, however, may be quite different. Because we're created free, we can freely choose to go to hell. We can throw away the gift and privilege of life by spending our days as if they don't matter—as if our time on earth is a joke that we, above all, do not take seriously. We can accumulate bling. We can intend more harm than good. We can use people and love things, instead of the other way around. We can believe in ourselves or our own impeccable morality more than we believe in God, divine mercy, and forgiveness.

I've sat in parish meetings where questions are raised about candidates for the sacraments. Is this child with severe cognitive limitations eligible to receive Eucharist meaningfully? Is this mentally ill homeless man a realistic catechumen for the RCIA? This young woman who's had several abortions and whose reputation is widely known: can she be successfully grafted into parish life here? This gay man, this couple with five past marriages between them, this former priest who wants to be our organist: what are we to do with these people?

God so loves the world that Jesus comes to the rescue *for them*, every one of them. If our doubts or scruples are stronger than our confidence in God's love and mercy, that says nothing about God—and a lot about us.

Idea of the Day

Am I comfortable with the idea that God wants to rescue all of us? Am I clear that some may refuse that rescue— but that doesn't give me the right to withhold it?

Renew

Anyone united with the Messiah gets a fresh start, is created new.
The old life is gone; a new life burgeons! Look at it!

2 Corinthians 5:17

When the hair's not right, we go for a makeover.
When the clothes don't fit, we head for the mall. When the job
begins to itch, we start scanning Craig's List. If we've outgrown
the apartment, we brake for Open Houses.

So why don't we as neatly ditch old patterns of behavior that
no longer contribute to the new person we're trying to become?
If I intend to quit drinking, I stop going to the bar and start going to AA. If I need to lose weight, the gym's a better destination

than Fatburgers. When companions are dragging me down, I make new friends with different interests. When family life is a source of endless conflict, it's time for a powwow, marriage counseling, or at least a renewed focus and applied energy. If I'm bored, disgusted, depressed, or angry all the time, I have to ask what's behind this dark season.

One sure way *not* to proceed is to gripe and moan and wish things were better. The Scarlett O'Hara approach—"I'll think about that, tomorrow!"—postpones trouble but doesn't solve it. Another resolve-killer is the blame game: if not for Mom, the boss, my spouse, or that teacher in the fifth grade, I'd be president of the United States by now....

Ultimately, the best way to trade in the life we don't want for the life we do is to change. For people of faith, change means to repent, confess, repair, and renew. We don't have to do this alone, and in fact we can't. Grace is what made it possible for Moses, murderer and stammerer, to become leader and lawgiver of Israel. Grace made a young Jewess of Nazareth the timeless Mother of God. It made Peter, fisherman, the foundation of a new assembly of faith. It made Paul of Tarsus, persecutor of Christians, the apostle to the Gentiles. Grace offers you and me—bit players on the stage of history—starring roles in the mission of the church, right where we are.

Idea of the Day

How well prepared am I to reap the harvest that grace is sowing in me? What can I do, or what must be done, so that new life burgeons in me?

Thank

I'm about to burst with song;
I can't keep quiet about you.
GOD, my God, I can't thank you enough.

PSALM 30:12

**THE OTHER NIGHT I WALKED INTO THE VESTIBULE OF MY
PARISH CHURCH.** Right as you enter, there's a striking statue of
Our Lady of Guadalupe. She's dark and lovely, usually wearing
a crown of fresh flowers someone has brought in thanksgiving.
At her feet are small gifts others have offered as tokens of joy
and love.

On this particular evening, none of these gentle details were first to impress upon me. What I saw was dirt. Dirt at the feet of the Madonna. Someone had tracked in fresh soil on his shoes and then left it there as a strange token of the visit. While not an intentional offering, it was quite obvious: a dark stain of two careless feet on the red carpet.

It rankled me. I'm not a fussy housekeeper, but in sacred space it bugs me when people don't take care. I'm the parishioner who goes around picking up stray bulletins left crumpled in pews. I remove cough drop wrappers from seat pockets. I've been known to scrape wads of gum off the floor. I'm a one-woman kneeler brigade, screwing loose kneelers into place so they don't bang during Mass. And as I'm retrieving the lollypop sticks and other junk left in the pews, I'm not always thinking nice thoughts about my fellow parishioners.

So my first response to Mr. Dirty Shoes was: *He might have wiped his feet before coming in here!* Then it occurred to me what those footprints represented. Someone had stood there, praying. Someone had come to church, fresh from gardening, or perhaps from a construction site, needing to pray more than he needed his dinner. He wasn't thinking about his shoes. He was thinking about his Blessed Mother. I was the one all wound up about the state of the carpet. He'd been concerned with matters of the heart.

So I stood there a little longer, thanking God for Mr. Dirty Shoes, for the lesson he taught me about what's important. I thanked Our Lady of Guadalupe for the interesting token received from her visitor that day. And then I cleaned it up.

Idea of the Day
How quick am I to ask for divine help, and how often do I stop to give thanks?

Immerse

By now it was a river over my head, water to swim in,
water no one could possibly walk through. He said,
"Son of man, have you had a good look?" **EZEKIEL 47:5–6**

THERE'S NOTHING LIKE BEING IN OVER YOUR HEAD TO GET YOU FOCUSED. I felt this way when I signed the contract on my first book. I was thrilled—and terrified. I went to bed for three weeks and couldn't keep a thing down for sheer nerves. Then I got up and started writing.

Years later, I was writing another book when the phone rang. I don't answer the phone when I'm working, which means I almost never answer the phone. But a friend's voice came through the answering machine, sounding upset. She said a mutual friend was in the hospital, suddenly paralyzed, inexplicably near death. Would I come?

I left my desk. I wouldn't return to it for eighteen months. Sometimes love leaves us no choice but to get in over our heads. I didn't know when I picked up the phone that day that I would wind up in the I.C.U. accepting power of attorney for a dying friend. I didn't really know what power of attorney meant. Or dying, for that matter. I just did what seemed necessary to do. I didn't know I would become the primary caregiver for a paralyzed friend. Or that such a proposition would involve more than time, organization, and paperwork. It would also mean dying to the person I was and becoming someone stronger, tougher, willing to fight pitch battles with the health care industry. It meant being reinvented as an unlikely lioness for the rights of a frail and defenseless man who couldn't speak for himself. In the space of a few weeks caring for my friend, I hardly knew myself.

All of us baptized into Christ are baptized into water that goes way over our heads. We'll be invited down roads we would never seek for ourselves. We'll have opportunities to become people we didn't know were in us to be. We'll explore all the colors of passion, both sides of it, love and suffering. And we'll never be the same, and grateful for it.

Idea of the Week

When has my faith invited me into deeper waters? Where Have I learned to swim against currents that challenged my limits?

Relax

"Can a mother forget the infant at her breast, walk away from the baby she bore? But even if mothers forget, I'd never forget you—never." **ISAIAH 49:15**

WHEN I AGREED TO CARE FOR A SICK FRIEND FOR THE REST OF HIS LIFE, I DIDN'T KNOW HOW LONG THAT WOULD BE. Or what was entailed. I knew at least it would mean dealing with hospitals, pharmacists, and specialists—territory I'd successfully avoided in my life until then. And I'd deal with them at their convenience, not mine. So I bought my first cell phone to be more available, and spread the number around on every form I filled out.

But I had to learn, at forty, how to be the sudden guardian of a sixty-four-year-old man. I visited the I.C.U. daily until my friend was moved to a nursing home. Then I was told this was temporary; I'd have to make other plans for him. He couldn't go home, since his house was wheelchair-impossible. So was my apartment. There was no money or time to make adjustments. Everything about his life, and mine, would have to change.

I spent the first weeks sleepless, anxious, moving my friend's belongings and mine into a third address, begging for money and help from every agency recommended to me. Then one afternoon as I hurried down the street toward yet another appointment, the cell phone rang in my pocket. I pulled it out, and an unfamiliar voice said, "Hello. I'm Doctor Breeman." I'd dealt with a half-dozen medical professionals so far, but not this one. Honestly, I didn't need another doctor right now. Yet the voice on the phone was smooth, mild, reassuring. He said, "I'm here for you. When you're ready, I'll walk you through what's happening, what's going to happen, what you can expect, what decisions you'll have to make, and what you'll need to do."

Legs trembling, I sat down on the sidewalk. I started to cry. I dearly needed a fairy godfather to show up in my life and tell me what to do. I was completely overwhelmed at becoming the unexpected custodian of my friend's end-of-life. Here was this stranger volunteering to be my guide. Everything was going to be all right. And it was.

Idea of the Day

Am I confident that God will take care of everything, even when I forget to ask? Do I live as if I believe God's care is real?

Intercede

God spoke to Moses, "Go! Get down there!
Your people whom you brought up from the land of Egypt
have fallen to pieces." **EXODUS 32:7**

LIFE IS A FRAGILE PROPOSITION. From the moment we're conceived, this life is imperiled by forces we can't control. Later, in the driver's seat of our existence, things get even more precarious. There seems to be no end to the way human beings can pursue their own destruction, risking the well-being of others in the process.

And in our vulnerability, we criticize those who seem to pose a threat to us, to what we love and value. Our leaders make that an easy option. So do our nation's rivals and enemies, the boss, coworkers, neighbors, friends, and strangers. We can dissect and disapprove of family members too. Or we can intercede for them all. It may be a new role for us, but it certainly has better results than judgment and condemnation.

The role of intercessor was awkward for Moses, mostly because he agreed with God: this nation God had led out of Egypt was a yoke and a burden! But discarding them was a waste of materials, not to mention a serious contradiction to the kind of Deity that God was supposed to be. Better to stick with them, then, and be true to the Divine self in the bargain. So Moses makes the argument. God relents. The Golden Calf Incident is overlooked.

We have an obligation to pray for our leaders whether we like them or not, and especially when we don't like them at all. We pray that they may be wise in their discernments, putting the common good above personal ambition. We pray for world leaders, particularly the bad ones, to repent their ways and care for their people. We pray for companies that consider the common good in their bottom line, that they may be blessed. And for corporations that exploit and pollute, that their hearts and ways might be changed. Jesus advises us to bless and not curse our enemies; interceding for them is one way to do that. And while we're praying for everyone who bugs us, it's good for us too. Harboring the spirit of blessing brings a blessing home to us.

Idea of the Week

Am I more inclined to bless or to curse? How do my intentions toward others shape the nature of my own heart?

Ask

Is anyone crying for help? GOD is listening, ready to rescue you.

Psalm 34:17

The willingness to ask for directions is a telling personality indicator. Despite the popular gender slam, the inability to ask isn't restricted to men. A certain kind of person finds this hard to do. It's about the need to be right or self-reliant, to avoid appearing weak or needy, not trusting others; it's about the conviction that everyone else knows less than you do; or it's just simple stubbornness. But when you're lost, you're lost. To get un-lost, you need help from someone who has more information than you do.

I get lost a lot, so I consider myself a resident expert on how to be found. I wear bright colors, tell everyone where I'm going, make friends along the way, purchase and carry and consult maps. All along the route, I ask fellow travelers: will this road really take me to X? Will there be water there, a hot dog stand, flush toilets? I've learned from experience not to rely too much on all those little symbols on the map. Just because it says there's a concession stand and restrooms is no reason not to bring trail mix and your own toilet paper.

Asking for help, or a little fact-check, shouldn't feel like defeat. Wanting to be right is only a problem if you can't accept being wrong. With no natural sense of direction, I'm proven wrong so often I feel quite flexible on this point. I offer opinions rather than manifestos, since chances are I'll have to revise and revisit the opinion at a later date. I can't avoid seeming weak or needy: I *am* weak and needy. For all these reasons, asking for advice, encouragement, or spiritual direction doesn't create an identity crisis.

All of this is good practice for seeking the ultimate bailout: from God. A few sessions of Humble 101 prepares us for spending time on our knees. A regular examination of conscience and visits to the confession room also keep us apprised of the truth about ourselves. If we need to be found, we have to begin by admitting we're lost.

Idea of the Day

Does the road I'm on have a map? From which sources do I seek direction and help? I dedicate my abstinence today to the possibility that I may be wrong about something I feel sure of.

Listen

"Let's get rid of the preacher.
That will stop the sermons!
Let's get rid of him for good.
He won't be remembered for long."

JEREMIAH 11:19B

I YELL AT YOU. You yell at me. I call you a name. You call me another. I punch you in the face. You punch me in the face. I put a curse on your people. You put a curse on mine. I raise an army and fight your clan. You raise an army and fight mine. I kill. You kill.

When is it all going to stop? One side has to refuse the challenge. One has to turn the other cheek. One of us has to absorb the offense without retaliation or escalation. There have been far too few Gandhis, Kings, and Mandelas. Most of the world seeks revenge, swift and decisive. Which is particularly troubling because revenge has historically never solved the problem.

History is a record of paybacks that backfired. The most ridiculous vengeance is the kind taken against words. When a book is denounced, more people read it. When an idea is banned, the idealists become an underground revolution. When a spokesperson is killed, people enshrine the words along with the memory. You can't kill a word. Words become flesh and live among us.

The enemies of the prophets try to silence them, for all the good it does. Amos was slain at a shrine in northern Israel where he delivered his message. Isaiah was executed by his king. Ezekiel was killed in exile in Babylon. Jeremiah was kidnapped and murdered by his countrymen in Egypt. Habakkuk was stoned in Jerusalem. Zechariah was murdered in the Temple. John the Baptist was beheaded in a fortress near the Dead Sea. And Jesus was crucified at Golgotha. All killed to shut them up.

What good did it do? We still know their names and what they did. We still read their words and proclaim them in our assemblies. Violence is a poor and useless weapon against an idea.

Idea of the Day

Lord, your word is alive and cannot be silenced. Give me ears to hear what you are saying to me through your Scriptures and your preachers, in your church, and especially in the lives of the disadvantaged ones.

Live!

You don't have to wait for the End. I am, right now,
Resurrection and Life. **John 11:25**

Every once in a while I catch myself doing it.
Coasting. Not living. I hunker down into routines, mindlessly
fixing meals, going to work, doing laundry, zoning out on the
couch. I start having the same conversations with the same people. I recycle the same thoughts and emotions. It's like someone
hit the pause button on my life and I stop growing.

It's not necessary to stop growing just because you're a certain
age, or you live alone, or because you have routines that can't be
avoided. Living boldly doesn't mean giving up preparing supper

for the kids! Every day of life is an opportunity to learn, love, and become more. We all take a time-out now and then, to mourn loss or absorb change. Sometimes we just forget we're alive and switch to autopilot. But when we wake up from this dormant stage, it's our privilege and our challenge to get back out there and get on with the business of living. Beauty awaits. Love beckons. Need tugs at our compassion. Adventure offers new companions and experiences. There are things we don't know yet, marvels we haven't witnessed, friends we haven't made, virtues we haven't cultivated.

Lazarus enters the tomb when he's dead, not of his own volition. An illness carried him off; friends and family buried him. But he emerges at the call of the Lord. No act of will on the part of Lazarus brings him back to life. He responds to the divine summons to come out of there! The times when our lives seem to go on screen saver are not usually conscious choices. Often events just speed up and we lose track of the forest because we're forced to dodge all the trees. At other times, we may actually crawl into the tomb and roll the stone in place from the inside. Not because we really want to: we're just out of breath, out of ideas, out of motivation. We need downtime from the toughness and the tragedy that is part of living.

However we get into the tomb, there's one sure way out: answering the call of the Lord of Life.

Idea of the Day

How alive am I at this stage in my life? How might I breathe more deeply the life offered to me?

Surrender

In the same way, anyone who holds on to life
just as it is destroys that life.
But if you let it go, reckless in your love,
you'll have it forever, real and eternal.

JOHN 12:25

MAYBE YOU'RE A PERSON WHO NEVER NEEDS TO BE COAXED INTO DOING SOMETHING BOLD OR RECKLESS. Are you first on the dance floor, last to leave the party? Do you dive off the board and check if there's water in the pool on the way down? Do you volunteer for every committee blindfolded, eagerly tuck into foods you've never heard of, travel to exotic destinations, fall in love with beautiful strangers?

I'm not recommending any of these behaviors, nor is the gospel. It's reckless *love* that's on the table, and not exactly the romantic kind. While life in this world is a unique and precious gift, it's not the only or the final value. Some things really are worth dying for. Sometimes the only bet worth placing is the entire farm.

If this idea troubles you, ask the people who've done it. Talk to missionaries, priests and sisters, folks in cloisters, and inquire if reckless love was worth the sacrifices they made and continue to make. Talk to lifelong married couples and ask if total fidelity was the right choice in the end. Ask dedicated parents if having children was a good idea. Ask retired teachers if they're glad for the years in the classroom. Ask artists if the uncertainties of their trade are compensated by the privilege to create. Read the words of the saints to see if they thought gambling on God turned out all right.

For most of us, getting to the heart of these words from Jesus about letting go of life in order to possess more of it can best be understood through our experiences of love. Love has such a staggering undertow from the moment we fall under its spell. All at once, those eyes across the room have the power to glue us to the spot and make us sing silly love songs. A newborn's red and wrinkly face is the irresistible new center of our world. A grandchild's hug makes our jaded hearts do flip-flops. Genuine love is always reckless. We die for it, every time.

Idea of the Week

When have I bet the farm on love, and did the gains match the losses?

FIFTH SUNDAY OF LENT (YEAR C)

Discard

*Yes, all the things I once thought were so important
are gone from my life. Compared to the high privilege of knowing
Christ Jesus as my Master, firsthand, everything I once thought
I had going for me is insignificant.* **PHILIPPIANS 3:8**

**IN THE 1970S A TOY WAS INTRODUCED TO CAPTIVATE
THE HEARTS OF LITTLE GIRLS.** It was called The Imagination
Dollhouse, and I wanted it. It had three cantilevered floors in
bright plastic colors, vanloads of put-together furniture, a small
70s-style nuclear family, and endless possibilities of setting up
the ultimate floor plan in a plastic universe of consumer joy.

My parents, unused to supplying their not-small or nuclear

family with everything hawked in TV ads, assured me I wouldn't be getting The Imagination Dollhouse for Christmas. It was too expensive; I was too old; it just wasn't happening. Still, on Christmas morning, nestled under the tree was a box so big, it could only be one thing. The dollhouse! I played with it all day, and had to be coaxed away from it to eat the holiday feast. Within a week, however, the toy went back in the box, and I never looked at it again. My parents had been right. I was too old.

The blatant consumer impulse behind that toy and others like it is something we're all too old for in this advanced millennium. Still, at this moment, I'm surrounded by things I was tempted to buy because of a sale price, perceived need, or simple boredom. My apartment is a shrine to buyer's remorse. Our regret for what we've done or failed to do goes beyond material purchases. In the moral universe, too, we experience buyer's remorse when we eat or drink too much, when we misuse our power, sexuality, or talents, or when we get what we asked for but not what we need. The Imagination Dollhouse was always better in my imagination than in all its plastic reality. That's proved to be true about a lot of things.

Once a woman accused of adultery was brought before Jesus. A man was involved too: we don't know the circumstances or motivations of either party. Needless to say, the dream had been different from the outcome. The mob's solution is to dispose of the woman. Jesus prefers to dispose of the offense. Compassion teaches better than stones.

Idea of the Day

What lessons have I learned by means of punishments?
What have I learned through mercy?

Terrify

"Eternal God, you who know all secrets,
who knew everything before it was something, you know that
these men brought false testimony against me....But I've done
none of the things they accuse me of. They made it all up!"

DANIEL 13:42B–43

LIBEL IS A SIN GRAVE ENOUGH TO MAKE THE TOP TEN COMMANDMENTS. Since words have the authority to create reality—as they do in the early moments of Genesis—they also have the power to invent fiction. A lie spoken out loud is released into the world like the contents of Pandora's box, unlikely to be re-contained. If only we could appreciate the great influence of the words we speak—opinions, criticisms, gossip, prejudice, cynicism, jeering, swearing, and misinformation—the world might be a quieter place.

The elders in Susanna's tale conspire to bear false witness against her. A woman will die unless the lie is exposed. This story is especially chilling because we know women may die in some countries today if men denounce them, rightly or wrongly. But we can't keep the horror at arm's length: in our own country, suspicion bears its own false witness, leading to so-called crimes of passion, lynchings, and hate crimes against houses of worship, personal property, and vulnerable human beings.

Big violence in the world begins with the tiny violence of the casual thought. "I have no use for those people." "I could just smack her." "His kind don't deserve justice." As we dismiss the humanity of an individual or group, we lay the brickwork for the false witness of bias and bigotry.

It's important to avoid giving false witness unwittingly, by repeating hearsay or capitalizing on media hype. After all, a for-profit news outlet is just as capable of massaging the truth into an artful deceit as you and I are. But beyond the mandate to avoid libel, we also have the responsibility to testify to the truth when the occasion demands it. If we don't speak up for vulnerable Susanna, who will?

Idea of the Day

Do I participate in conversations in which put-downs are the norm and accusations are implied? Do I remain silent when truth is mangled, or do I object and correct?

Transcend

Jesus said, "You're tied down to the mundane;
I'm in touch with what is beyond your horizons.
You live in terms of what you see and touch.
I'm living on other terms." **JOHN 8:23**

WHEN I WAS FIVE, I HAD A STRONG DESIRE TO BECOME A LOUNGE SINGER. I must have seen too many black-and-white movies in which such a person reclined on top of a piano in a sparkly gown and crooned a song. It seemed like a wonderful occupation! However, by the time I was seven and well into parochial school, I wanted to be like the Sisters I admired so much. At nine, after penning my first story, I hoped to write the great American novel. At twelve, I anticipated a career as a university professor.

None of the early dreams for my life came true. And in another sense, all of them did. I wound up serving the church as a lay minister, and enjoying a teaching career as a catechist. I write for a living. And, at least metaphorically, I get to sing the great song of salvation in the work I do. But I rarely get to wear the sparkly dress and have yet to recline on a piano.

Our early dreams are tied to the world we see around us. We want to be mommies or daddies, teachers or firefighters, or movie stars like the people on TV. What else do we know? A lot of Catholic adults admit to having played Mass as children. Married business owners tell me their daughter never played house, but liked to play office.

Any honest work can be consecrated work, if surrendered to holy purposes. We don't always feel that way about our daily tasks. Does it serve God when I wash dishes and vacuum carpets? Does it fulfill the mission of the church when I make deadline on a project? What's so consecrated about running errands, or holy about paying bills? Often it's not the nature of a task that makes it holy, but the spirit in which we submit to the labor, the dedication we invest, the way we treat those around us, and the integrity we bring to everything we do. Start with a conscious self-offering, and let God take it from there.

Idea of the Day

God, it's all yours—all of it! Everything I think and say and do and intend. Guide my heart and my hands today to your holy purposes.

Refuse

"Is it true, Shadrach, Meshach, and Abednego, that you don't respect my gods and refuse to worship the gold statue that I have set up? I'm giving you a second chance—but from now on, when the big band strikes up you must go to your knees and worship the statue I have made." **DANIEL 3:14-15A**

FOR SHEER THEATER, THE GOLDEN CALF INCIDENT IN EXODUS IS MEMORABLE. A bored, anxious community at the foot of Sinai creates an image to match their hopes for a strong, take-no-prisoners kind of god. Meanwhile, Moses is on the mountaintop, working out fine points of moral legislation for the new nation. Which God would you choose: the one you just worship, or One who wants your obedience?

The allure of the golden calf never dies in Israel. It's resurrected in the promised land, when an Israelite king erects two gold calves at the shrines of Dan and Bethel respectively to mark the borders of his kingdom. This northern king hopes to discourage his people from crossing the southern border to worship in Jerusalem's Temple. While these images weren't intended as rival gods to the One God of Israel, they certainly meant to define God's nature.

The God of Abraham, Isaac, Jacob, Moses, and the prophets is fundamentally a mystery. Not that God plays hard to get; if so, why reveal the divine Presence at all? Rather, the first commandment condemns image-making for its end result: defining God down to a thing to be worshipped, admired, and displayed. But not necessarily obeyed.

Flash forward to the story of Daniel's three noble friends. They don't care how long the band plays on, they are not going to bend the knee to a gold image. Their God is so much bigger than this! They will not play the game of reduction in matters of divinity. To reduce and contain God is to lose sight of God altogether.

A lot of well-meaning people will tell you precisely who God is. Unless it's Jesus you're talking to, don't take their construct as the last word on the subject. And above all, don't bend a knee to it! Let the band play on without you.

Idea of the Day

Holy God, you are Mystery and Trinity, source of love, life, compassion, beauty, and truth. Beyond this I am speechless. Reveal yourself to me.

Cling

"You're not even fifty years old—and Abraham saw you?"
"Believe me," said Jesus, "I am who I am long before Abraham
was anything." That did it—pushed them over the edge.

JOHN 8:57B–59A

**A LOT OF PEOPLE WE KNOW AND LOVE LEAVE THE
CHURCH.** They leave for reasons we appreciate and some we
don't. They walk away over issues that seem justifiable and others that sound superficial. They depart because of who they are,
and who or what they understand the church to be. Some exit
after great deliberation, and others walk off in an hour of exas-
peration. Some seventeen million U.S. Catholics don't worship

with us anymore. And we aren't permitted to stand in judgment over any of them. God alone judges hearts. It's our job to love and pray for our sisters and brothers—what we'd be doing even if they had remained in communion with us.

Dozens of people in my life have left the church. My sister became an atheist because of the hypocrisy she saw in church-going people. Another sister joined the Latter-Day Saints after falling in love with a man who is Mormon. My cousin is Lutheran today because he feels women should be ordained and priests should marry. My nephew became Evangelical as a result of a particular priest's harsh treatment of him. Many good friends walked away because of church teaching on homosexuality. Others cashed in their Catholic ID after the clerical scandal of child sexual abuse and the way some bishops handled it. Some left because Vatican II was too radical; others because it wasn't radical enough. To be honest, I know quite a few former Catholics who just found going to church really boring and meaningless. It didn't seem to help or matter.

If you're entertaining an exit strategy, for reasons above or others uniquely your own, I'd like to invite you to stay. Here, in this church, as church, with me. Not because of me, but because of the Jesus who formed this church with his own body. There are lots of reasons to leave the church, and only one to remain: the Jesus who asks us to remain in him like branches on a vine. People can be stinkers, parishes found wanting, and institutions darn frustrating—wherever you go. Jesus is the same, yesterday, today, and forever.

Idea of the Day

What is my attitude toward "retired" Catholics? What makes church hopeful to me?

Lament

Then I hear whispering behind my back:
"There goes old 'Danger-Everywhere.' Shut him up! Report him!"
JEREMIAH 20:10

EVERY AUTHENTIC SPIRITUAL LIFE INCLUDES THE ELE-MENT OF LAMENTATION. All the saints do it. Teresa of Avila and John of the Cross practically created a school behind the practice. Even Jesus offers his lament from the cross: "My God, my God, why have you forsaken me?"

In Scripture, Jeremiah's the king of lamentation. "Holy complaining" fills a good portion of his book. When he's not actually prophesying, Jeremiah spends a lot of time whining about being a prophet. This makes him a member in good stead of the larger guild of writers of my acquaintance. Most writers, when they're not writing, are moaning about how tough the creative process is.

What separates the pedestrian whiners from the biblical lamenters is mostly the direction of the wail. Most complainers we know are having a pity party for themselves. The ticket to such a party reads: *Admit One*. If you actually listen to someone complain, it's as if you're eavesdropping. This isn't about you; it's about them! The practitioner of lament, by contrast, is having a dialogue with God. They're not happy with how things are going, and they expect God to do something about it.

This points out the second distinction between complainers and lamenters. Complainers are wallowing. They don't need your help for this and don't anticipate a rescue anyway. Just try to say something reassuring and see! Lamenters, however, seek and expect results. That's why they're talking to God. God is the only one who can help.

This brings us to the third facet of lamentation: faith. Whiners don't need faith to verbalize their despair. It's all about venting, expressing, releasing. It's a cathartic process, not a religious gesture. Lamentation requires the element of faith: sooner or later, the lament must bend in the direction of expressed confidence in God's past generosity, present concern, and future response. After lament, you let go and trust.

Idea of the Day

God, can complaining really be a holy occupation? Today, let me dedicate my abstinence to the issue that's bugging me the most.

Recommit

*"I'll make a covenant of peace with them that
will hold everything together, an everlasting covenant.
I'll make them secure and place my holy place of worship
at the center of their lives forever. I'll live right there with them.
I'll be their God! They'll be my people!"*

EZEKIEL 37:26–27

CONTRARY TO THE FAMILIAR SAYING, PROMISES ARE NOT MADE TO BE BROKEN. They're made to be kept. Fidelity can seem outdated in a faddish world that insists we change clothes, cars, phones, and hair styles in due season. We suffer from culture-wide attention disorder as media cycles leap from topic to topic.

Ideas start to smell fishy if you hold onto them longer than everyone else. In this environment of swift and sudden U-turns, how are we supposed to hold onto the *people* in our lives?

When change is fast and frequent, relationships suffer. Chasing an ever-shifting career path, we discover we don't know our spouse anymore. An embraceable child turns into a withdrawn adolescent. The friend we haven't seen in a while has undergone big life changes we know nothing about. Past mentors sicken and age and die while our backs are turned and attention is elsewhere. These things don't happen all in an hour. They've been happening for a long time and we didn't notice. Covenants ignored are easily misplaced.

Israel's covenant with God stood on four sturdy legs. First, there was the pledge of countless descendants; then, the land of promise; next, a kingship that would never end; and, finally, a temple where God would dwell with the people always. This covenant seemed secure until 587 BC, when Babylonians crashed through the walls of Jerusalem, destroyed the Temple, ended the monarchy, and dragged the community into exile. In one fell swoop, the four-point covenant was left teetering on a single leg. With Temple, kingship, and land suspended, all the community had left was its own survival.

How does Israel regain its trust in a God whose promises seemed made to be broken? By recognizing it was the community, not God, who failed the responsibilities of fidelity. Even in exile, the prophet Ezekiel begins unfolding the new covenant God holds out to Israel with both hands. God's promises are made to be renewed.

Idea of the Day

How many of my commitments need to be renewed? Am I a better promise-maker than a promise-keeper?

Palm Sunday of the Lord's Passion (Year A)

Pray

Going a little ahead, he fell on his face, praying,
"My Father, if there is any way, get me out of this. But please,
not what I want. You, what do you want?" **Matthew 26:39**

SUFFERING ISN'T TO BE SOUGHT FOR ITS OWN MERITS.
In past times, instruments of self-flagellation and "discipline"
appealed to Christians who desired fuller communion with the
crucified Lord and his martyrs. There are other ways to enjoy that
deeper identification. They involve the choices we make, some
of which may bring all the suffering we care to accept—but as a
by-product of greater goals, not as the goal itself. It's clear Jesus
isn't looking for suffering on the night before he dies. He doesn't

want it. Three gospels describe how he prays to avoid suffering that final night. If there's another way to achieve the divine will, Jesus would have personally preferred it.

This makes it awkward for those who claim it's "God's will" that anyone should suffer. While Jesus consecrates his suffering to holy purposes, he doesn't enshrine suffering itself as a wonderful thing. The message of the cross is not that it's holy to suffer, or that it's pleasing to God when we do. The cross tells us that God is willing to suffer—with us and for us. To harm ourselves, or to actively seek pain as a spiritual practice, is a dangerous way to miss the point.

Jesus approaches suffering the way you and I might do: by asking for a reprieve! At the same time, Jesus models what to do when suffering is, finally, unavoidable. He asks to understand what God wants from him in this hour. This is the most important prayer ever prayed. It's one you and I must keep in our pockets for when we need it—because we will need it. When loss and failure come to us, when illness and weakness, disability and dying are irrevocably in our path, we can pray for these things to pass us by in some miraculous way. But if they don't, we must also ask: You, God, what do you want? How can we use this inexorable event, harsh and cruel as it is, as a channel for your grace?

Idea of the Day

Which elements of my life have caused me the most suffering so far? Of what use has God made of them, or how might I consecrate their irrevocable reality to holy purposes from now on?

Doubt

*Peter blurted out, "Even if everyone else is ashamed of you
when things fall to pieces, I won't be."
Jesus said, "Don't be so sure."*

Mark 14:29–30a

**In the sixteenth century, Saint Philip Neri prayed
in a witty spirit that's become famous: "Lord, watch
over Philip today, for he will betray you!"** He perceived
plainly what the rest of us try to hide from: personal culpability. Saint
Philip knew well that while our faith in God should be total, belief
in ourselves should be closely examined.

Self-righteousness is a natural weed that grows in the gardens of
the faithful. We who go to church regularly, receive the sacraments

adequately, keep the commandments (most of them, most of the time), and nod vigorously at church teaching (some of it, much of the time) are easily tempted to think we've got this religion thing down to a science. We may even imagine we've got salvation in the bag! And why not? We're not bad people. We know what bad people look like, and we're not like that. We max out our charitable giving quota on our itemized taxable deductions each year. We never swear in front of children. Our neighbors think we're solid citizens. Our mothers think we're swell.

While faith is a good thing—one of three theological virtues, along with hope and love, according to Saint Paul—doubt can be useful too. Especially when it's directed at our own righteousness. Peter's big mistake at the Last Supper is to imagine that his loyalty to Jesus is invincible. Hasn't he been with Jesus since Galilee? Didn't he walk away from his nets at a moment's notice? Wasn't Peter the only one to give Jesus the right answer when asked, "Who do people say that I am?" Didn't he get out of the boat and (attempt to) walk on water? Wasn't Peter one of the chosen three who saw Jesus transfigured, who stood by him during fateful miracles, and who will soon be invited to pray with him in the garden? Doesn't all this prove that Jesus can count on Peter? Well, doesn't it?

Apparently not. Peter never sees his betrayal coming because he lacks the humility that self-knowledge requires. We can't afford to make the same mistake.

Idea of the Day

Who models the spirit of humility best for me? What practices help me to grow in this virtue?

Decide

*[Then Pilate said to them,] "You brought this man to me
as a disturber of the peace...It's clear that he's done nothing
wrong, let alone anything deserving death.
I'm going to warn him to watch his step and let him go."
At that, the crowd went wild: "Kill him! Give us Barabbas!"*

Luke 23:14a, 15b, 16, 18

In a climate of bullies, we're asked to be peacemakers. To a lot of good folks this is unrealistic. If people around us come out swinging, does it make sense to present our faces to be smashed? And yes, we know Jesus said the thing about turning the other cheek. Well, we're not going to. We're not patsies. We're

going to fight fire with fire and fists with fists. Besides, we're cultur-
ally conditioned to appreciate a good gunfight. So, in the choice
between the Prince of Peace and Barabbas, give us Barabbas.

The irony in the Passion story is that Jesus was surrendered to
the authorities as a *disturber* of the peace. The religious leaders
wanted him dead because he was a troublemaker. So in the choice
between Jesus and a terrorist, the leaders incited the crowds to
ask for the terrorist. Go figure.

In every assembly of Christians we find some who are curi-
ously trigger-happy. I'm not talking about guns here, but about
the decision for violent solutions to social problems. Many
churchgoers sincerely believe the way to deal with unwelcome
pregnancies is to sacrifice the child. Or that violent crime is re-
duced by executing violent criminals. And when terrorists roam
the earth, we're in our rights to become torturers. When people
come across our borders illegally to support their families, it's
justice to tear those families apart with deportation rather than
reward lawbreakers. An eye for an eye, a tooth for a tooth—and
a military response when it seems expedient.

In the seasonal choice between the man of peace and Barabbas,
we want Barabbas. He makes sense to us. He's a freedom fighter
against the Roman imperialists. Yes, he's a killing machine, but
killers can be useful. Besides, what good is a Prince of Peace?
Healers, teachers, and saints will not obliterate enemy forces! In
a world full of bullies, it's hard not to become one.

Idea of the Day

*God of peace, I am deeply troubled by the realities of living
in a violent world. I don't want to hurt anyone, but I don't
want to be hurt either. Show me the way.*

Terrify

Mary came in with a jar of very expensive aromatic oils, anointed and massaged Jesus' feet, and then wiped them with her hair. The fragrance of the oils filled the house. **JOHN 12:3**

EVEN BEFORE JESUS TEACHES THE LESSON, ONE OF HIS BEST STUDENTS DOES HER HOMEWORK. In Chapter 13, Jesus washes the feet of his friends as a lasting lesson in discipleship. Days earlier, however, Mary of Bethany kneels at his feet and performs this beautiful act of service. The gesture is so eloquent and intimate, it could have motivated Jesus to choose the sign of footwashing as his last instruction to his companions. Mary, accustomed to sitting at the feet of Jesus and receiving his

117

lessons, always was a pretty quick study.

Jesus appreciates the significance of the oils as a sign of his impending death. Lazarus sits at table with them that evening—"so recently raised from the dead," as John pointedly notes. These same oils may have been used to anoint Mary's brother not long ago. But Lazarus now lives while Jesus is imperiled, as Mary somehow intuits. Bethany is a short walk from Jerusalem. The talk in the city is surely wild enough after Sunday's dramatic and provocative entrance to go either way.

She therefore brings out the oils, demonstrating that she apprehends the danger, perceives the hour, and understands the need for preparation. Ironically, the only other person at table with Jesus that night who can say the same is Judas. The other disciples never did show a feel for the time. They never could embrace the risk. And they were always woefully unprepared.

One can't help but consider a "shadow twelve" alongside the officially counted ones: Mary of Nazareth. Peter's mother-in-law, who serves Jesus the moment she's healed. Mary Magdalene. Susanna and Joanna, providing for the disciples from their resources. Mary and Martha of Bethany. Mary, mother of James and John, and Salome, both faithful at the cross and tomb. The Syrophoenician mother who insists Jesus break his rules and cure her child. The hemorrhaging woman who's sure that touching Jesus will be enough to heal her. The anonymous woman who blesses the womb that bore Jesus when she hears his gospel. Some disciples really do their homework.

Idea of the Day

How do I demonstrate my service as a follower of Jesus?

Wait

But I said, "I've worked for nothing. I've nothing to show for a life of hard work. Nevertheless, I'll let GOD have the last word. I'll let him pronounce his verdict." **Isaiah 49:4**

AFTER READING THE BIOGRAPHY OF MOTHER FRANCES XAVIER CABRINI, I WAS READY TO RETIRE ANY CLAIM TO A PRODUCTIVE LIFE. This woman was a powerhouse! She crossed the ocean twenty-four times (at the turn of the nineteenth century, on ships, through storms!), opening sixty-seven schools, hospitals, and orphanages in Europe, Central and South America, and the United States. She didn't take no for an answer from bishops or politicians—and all this in an era when women couldn't vote, Italian immigrants were despised, and Catholics weren't welcome in many countries, including ours. The thing that kills me is: Mother Cabrini was sick the whole time she was sailing around missionizing the world.

If you want to feel small and irrelevant, compare yourself with Frances Cabrini. But then get over yourself. Sainthood is not baseball. It's not about the statistics. Yes, Cabrini wrangled the financing for sixty-seven charitable institutions in countries where she didn't even speak the language. I couldn't open a hot dog stand across the street to save my life. She performed miracles, and I struggle to make deadlines. She crossed oceans; I rarely leave the apartment without a good reason. We can go on like this all day, but the bottom line is, none of it matters. Maybe it matters to me, a little, but what really counts is what God says about it in the final analysis.

While I'm tempted to pronounce a quick postmortem on my Christian contribution, I'm obliged to hesitate. This is because Isaiah—the greatest Hebrew prophet of them all, the gifted writer-poet who makes the rest of the Old Testament read like a tenth-grade term paper!—says he has nothing to show for his life. He. Isaiah. And then, he admits that God alone gets to judge these things.

If Isaiah can wait for God to pass judgment on his contribution, then so must I. This means returning to the tiny field assigned to me and continuing the harvest. Discouragement tempts me every day, and yet I resist. I can't see as God does.

Idea of the Day

Gracious God, I humbly ask to become the smallest of your saints. Obscurity is fine, so long as you get the harvest assigned to my care.

Encourage

The Master, GOD, has given me a well-taught tongue,
So I know how to encourage tired people. **ISAIAH 50:4A**

SAINT PAUL ADMITS THAT NOT ALL OF US ARE CUT OUT TO BE APOSTLES. We may not be prophets, teachers, or healers either. Most of us don't speak in tongues. But all are summoned to service in the Body of Christ. No exceptions.

We each get the same gifts of the Spirit to enable us for our task. You may remember the "big seven" gifts of Confirmation: wisdom, understanding, knowledge, counsel, fortitude, reverence, and wonder in the presence of God. We each produce the same fruits of the Spirit as the harvest of these graces put to use.

The "big nine" fruits are: love, joy, peace, patience, kindness, generosity, faithfulness, gentleness, and self-control. What remains ours to choose is the nature of our service. That depends on our status in life: young or old, single or married or under religious vows, parenting or empty-nesting, employed or retired or somewhere in between. Our personal resources and skills come into play. We offer what we have in thanks for what we've received.

I know a religious sister forced to retire due to ill health. She can no longer pursue the work that consumed her life until now. One day while riding the bus, Sister noticed how much weariness, sadness, and hopelessness many of the faces around her displayed. Eyes seemed hard with mistrust, or empty from depression. Suddenly she found her new service. She calls it "the ministry of benevolent glances." Every day now she rides the bus, gazing at each of the faces with softness, compassion, and tenderness. If someone looks up, she smiles at that person with warmth and encouragement. Often they smile back, a bit surprised to be noticed at all. With benevolent glances, this Sister continues to make her life a blessing for others.

We're often in situations where we don't know what to say. So we babble, multiplying words to cover the silence and embarrassment. While that may help in some circumstances, at other times it's only self-serving. Less can be more. What people really need is to read our eyes and know we care.

Idea of the Day

Lord, teach me serve you with a well-trained tongue. But when words are not helpful, give me soft eyes to lend comfort and assurance.

Remember

What you must solemnly realize is that every time you eat this bread and every time you drink this cup, you reenact in your words and actions the death of the Master. You will be drawn back to this meal again and again until the Master returns.

1 CORINTHIANS 11:26

THERE'S A TABLE AT THE CENTER OF OUR LIVES. From it we Catholics take our meaning and purpose. This table demands something of us as well—that we're prepared to give up our lives to each other in response to the meal we share.

Christianity is extreme religion. It's not meant to be a sweet, pious coating around a civil, moral, decent life. When you have a crucified man in the middle of your religion, you can expect that much is expected. When you have a crucified God at the center of your worship, you have to know that pieties and niceties won't be enough. Christianity is not spiritual whitewash over an ordinary existence. It penetrates bone and marrow and requires deep, soul-shattering transformation. Our faith is something to live for and to die for. It has ramifications for now and for eternity.

Which is why we return again and again to this table at the center of our lives. Dessert is not served here. This is a costly meal of flesh and blood. We take the life of Jesus Christ into our bodies. We are taken into his Body with the same gesture. Christ offers himself and we offer ourselves. It's an extraordinary decision we make, and it has vital consequences for everything else we do and intend.

See you at Supper.

Idea of the Day

Self-giving God, I approach your Eucharist with open eyes, with my whole heart, and with fear and trembling. Christ comes to me. I go to Christ.

Love

[Pilate said,] "Are you the 'King of the Jews'?"
"My kingdom," said Jesus, "doesn't consist of what you see around
you. If it did, my followers would fight so that I wouldn't
be handed over...But I'm not that kind of king,
not the world's kind of king." **JOHN 18:33, 36**

PASSION IS A DOUBLE-EDGED SWORD. IT INVOLVES LOVE AND SUFFERING. We all want love. We all fear suffering. Yet who has ever loved and not suffered for its sake?

When we love, we sign an implicit contract with the realm of suffering. We embrace more than just the beloved. We embrace the future that the decision to love brings into being. We make declarations of intent: "in good times and in bad, for richer, for poorer, in sickness and in health, till death do us part." Naturally, we pin our hopes on good times, riches, and health. But we're not so foolish as to imagine that bad times won't come along for the ride. Fortunes rise and fall. Illness can't be warded off forever. And death *is* on the horizon of every human life. Death is the horizon. Human love is a wonderful, powerful thing. But it doesn't change the terms of our mortality.

Only divine love can do that. And divine love *has* done that, through the willing passion of Jesus. Jesus is the king who didn't have to suffer and die, but chose it as a lasting sign of God's total presence and stake in human misery. God is nailed to our suffering. God weeps with our grief. God cries out in our affliction. God dies inside our death. In the times of our greatest need, there is no absence. There is total presence, what we call Real Presence. As humanity suffers, God is here, suffering with us. This is what love does.

If Jesus were the world's sort of king, he'd hold himself above and apart from its sadness. But in the reign of God, which is a realm of love, the only place to be is with the beloved. The cross is passionately staked to the spot of our mortality, and it becomes the wondrous ladder of our rescue.

Idea of the Day

Passionate God, with my fast today I commit to you all the sorrows of my heart and at the heart of this broken world. Mend what is broken, heal what is wounded, and save what is lost.

Rejoice!

They found the entrance stone rolled back from the tomb, so they walked in. But once inside, they couldn't find the body of the Master Jesus. **LUKE 24:1–3**

THE TOMB IS EMPTY. What does empty mean? It's an absence in want of a presence. Emptiness seeks fullness, begs to be assigned meaning. Every Easter we approach the tomb and find it empty. What meaning do we assign to this?

We can say Jesus was taken by his enemies and we don't know where they've put him. We can say Jesus was taken by his friends and hidden to create an intriguing mystery. We can say Jesus was never there at all. Or we can say he is risen from the dead and lives.

If we say Jesus lives! then we also say something very significant about emptiness, absence, and want. We assign new meaning to empty places like loss, longing, loneliness. We assign new dimensions and possibilities even to death! We redefine hope from within our hopeless mortality. And we say something extraordinary about the God in whom we place our trust.

What we believe as we stand in the emptiness of the tomb shapes everything we hold true about reality. If we say He is Risen! then we're ready to stand in all the lonely places, with all the longing and suffering people. And there, even there, we'll find the courage to rejoice.

Idea of the Day
Jesus lives. In me. Now what?